Working together for healthy young minds

A practitioner's workbook

Steven Walker

Russell House Publishing

First published in 2003 by:
Russell House Publishing Ltd.
4 St. George's House
Uplyme Road
Lyme Regis
Dorset DT7 3LS
Tel: 01297-443948
Fax: 01297-442722
e-mail: help@russellhouse.co.uk
www.russellhouse.co.uk

British Library Cataloguing-in-publication Data:
A catalogue record for this book is available from the British Library.

ISBN: 1-903855-26-8

Design and layout by Jeremy Spencer, London.

Printed by Cromwell Press, Trowbridge.

About Russell House Publishing

RHP is a group of social work, probation, education and youth and community work practitioners and academics working in collaboration with a professional publishing team. Our aim is to work closely with the field to produce innovative and valuable materials to help managers, trainers, practitioners and students. We are keen to receive feedback on publications and new ideas for future projects. For details of our other publications please visit our website or ask us for a catalogue. Contact details are on this page.

Contents

Acknowledgements

My grateful thanks to colleagues and children and adolescents with whom I have worked over the years in a variety of contexts, all of whom have contributed to my thinking and practice in the area of child and adolescent mental health. A special thanks to Geoffrey Mann and Martin Calder at Russell House Publishing for encouraging me to complete this workbook which developed from my previous book on the subject of child and adolescent mental health. Martin Jones and Jeremy Spencer have done an excellent job with editing and design. My wife Isobel and daughter Rose deserve the biggest thanks because their love and support have provided me with a constant emotional anchor in life's turbulent seas, whilst they have endured my preoccupation with and the distractions of, concentrated manuscript production.

Steven Walker
Winter 2002

About the author

Steven Walker is a senior lecturer in the School of Community Health and Social Studies, Anglia Polytechnic University. He has worked directly with children and families for 18 years in child protection and child and adolescent mental health contexts. He is a UKCP registered family psychotherapist and a member of the Institute for Learning and Teaching in Higher Education.

Also by Steven Walker from Russell House Publishing:

– **Social Work and Child and Adolescent Mental Health** (2003).

– with Jane Akister, **Social Work and Family Therapy** (forthcoming).

– **Social Work Assessment and Intervention** (forthcoming).

Dedication

To Mam and Dad

Introduction

Evidence of the rising numbers and specific characteristics of child, adolescent, and young people's mental health problems has been thoroughly documented, prompting widespread professional, public and private concern. Social and health care practitioners in every agency are at the heart of this phenomenon working in the front line where children, families, parent/carers, schools and communities are experiencing the destructive consequences.

The need to develop child and adolescent mental health services, (CAMHS) has attracted more attention in recent years due to increased demands on specialist resources by parents, youth workers, teachers, social workers, and primary health care staff. Attempting to meet the needs of children and young people from the ages of four in nurseries through to 24-year-old rough sleepers suffering emotional and behavioural problems as well as their carers/families, has proved onerous. The evidence has suggested the need for policy and practice changes to ensure a sufficient range of provision and skills to improve the effectiveness and efficiency of CAMHS.

Recent studies from several different countries agree fairly closely that the prevalence of mental health problems in children up to the age of 18 years is 10 per cent. There are higher rates among groups that suffer a number of risk factors such as those who live in many poor, inner city environments and young adults in the age range 15-25 years. It is estimated that in Britain, one in five children and young people manifest mild emotional or behavioural difficulties or the early stage of significant problems that do not require long- term specialist intervention. However, only a small proportion of these children actually present to services for help, manifesting difficulties in a variety of contexts where the cause of the problem is not adequately addressed. Many staff lack confidence in assessing and intervening even when they suspect a mental health component to the difficulties being presented.

This book aims to provide a resource for practitioners in a variety of contexts in voluntary or statutory agencies who may encounter situations where concerns are expressed about the behaviour, emotional state, or mental health of a child or young person. This could be in child protection, primary care, young offenders, family support, long-term planning, youth work, paediatric nursing, fostering and adoption, juvenile justice, education, probation and, of course, child and adolescent mental health services. The workbook aspires to provide a foundation of theoretical ideas and practical guidance that will offer support in an accessible and challenging format to create the basis for informed, reflective, confident practice.

Working in the field of child and adolescent mental health is an awesome undertaking. It covers the majority of the most intense and rapidly changing periods of human growth and development, within which are laid the foundations for much of what will transpire in the rest of a person's life. Your contribution is therefore crucial bringing as it does a professional dimension to a child or young person's emotional and behavioural experience at a time when effective intervention can make a difference for the present and in the future. I have sought to provide a varied menu to choose from of accessible and useful resources and information gleaned from contemporary sources of evidence-based literature and quality research, as well as from my own experience in CAMHS work. These are designed to be applied in whatever context you practice, from primary through to specialist levels of support in voluntary or statutory agencies.

Content of workbook

The workbook is designed as a practical manual for use by busy practitioners requiring evidence-based knowledge and guidance to enable you to engage with children, adolescents, young people and their families in a supportive context.

It aims to help you engage with the needs and agenda of children and young people who are troubled. Twenty-four activities throughout the six chapters are designed to stimulate your reflective capacity and together with the practice guidance, offer you resources to bring to bear on the difficulties faced by your clients or service users. This book covers the wider policy and legal context of child and adolescent mental health problems and how services for this group of young people are organised and delivered. Definitions and prevalence of various mental health problems are elucidated and underpinned by contemporary quantitative data concerning signs, symptoms and resilience factors. Practice guidance will illuminate the crucial area of assessment and the different contexts in which children and adolescents become vulnerable to developing mental health problems.

Culturally competent practice is described and discussed in order to distinguish the particular needs of a diverse multi-cultural and ethnically rich society. Methods and models of intervention, and their underpinning theories are systematically organised to offer a broad repertoire of helping strategies to aid practitioner skill development. The importance of multi-disciplinary and interprofessional care is explored to help locate your practice within the appropriate network of statutory and voluntary resources to fulfil the aim of holistic support.

Partnership practice and service user evaluation is a growing area of interest in practice. This concept is developed and applied to the area of child and adolescent mental health in the final chapter to illustrate the potential of an empowering, child-focused design and delivery of effective services that meets the needs and responds to the agenda of young people themselves. Finally, a selected list of organisations that can offer resources directly or indirectly in child and adolescent mental health that are accessible to children and young people themselves or for parents and practitioners has been included.

Learning outcomes

1. Contribute to the understanding and assessment of the mental health needs and problems of children, adolescents and young people.

2. Communicate and engage with young people in a process of partnership practice that enables them to identify and articulate their needs and agendas.

3. Demonstrate critical understanding of current policy and legal aspects of working with children, young people, and their families.

4. Demonstrate knowledge and awareness of the importance of culturally competent practice.

5. Communicate effectively in partnership with multi-disciplinary staff in delivering the care needs of children, adolescents and their families.

6. Contribute to the effective planning and use of methods and models of intervention with clients.

7. Demonstrate knowledge of the requirements for evidence-based practice and the importance of effective evaluation.

Learning profile

On the following pages is a list of the **learning objectives** you will need to attain in order to demonstrate the learning outcomes for each chapter outlined above. You can use it to evaluate your current understanding of child and adolescent mental health practice, and to help you decide how the workbook can help you extend this. The profile is for your general guidance only; you might like to use it particularly in the early stages of your learning, or for further professional development in planning with peers and your employer.

For each of the objectives listed below, please tick the box on the scale that most closely corresponds to your present knowledge. You can use this to determine in how much detail you will need to study each chapter. At the end of the book you will find an identical list of objectives and the same scale – by completing this Learning Review you can gauge how much your learning has developed and on what areas you still need to work.

Chapter 1: Multi-disciplinary working

	Not at all	Partly	Very well

I can:

	Not at all	Partly	Very well
Explain the importance of multi-disciplinary working	❏	❏	❏
Describe the obstacles to, and ways to achieve effective multi-disciplinary work	❏	❏	❏
Describe how changing patterns of service delivery are influencing professional relationships	❏	❏	❏
Work in partnership to identify and analyse potential problems and appropriate responses	❏	❏	❏

Chapter 2: Definitions, prevalence and assessment

I can:

	Not at all	Partly	Very well
Describe the differences between mental health, mental health problem, and mental disorder	❏	❏	❏
Explain the importance of theories of human growth and development	❏	❏	❏
Describe risk and resilience factors in children and young people	❏	❏	❏
Understand how knowledge, skills and values are integrated in effective assessment	❏	❏	❏

Chapter 3: Culturally competent practice

	Not at all	Partly	Very well
I can:			
Describe what is meant by culturally competent practice	❑	❑	❑
Illustrate the importance of cultural identity to the mental health of a diverse society	❑	❑	❑
Explain how understanding of oppression and discrimination influences contemporary practice	❑	❑	❑
Understand the mental health needs of black and ethnic minority families	❑	❑	❑

Chapter 4: The organisational and legal context

	Not at all	Partly	Very well
I can:			
Describe the four tier model of CAMHS organisation	❑	❑	❑
Describe the main legislative framework for CAMHS	❑	❑	❑
Explain how CAMHS fits with other children's services	❑	❑	❑
Identify how different agencies conceptualise children and young people's mental health problems	❑	❑	❑

Chapter 5: Planning and intervention

	Not at all	Partly	Very well
I can:			
Integrate knowledge, skills and values in analysing information and weighing its significance and priority	❏	❏	❏
Demonstrate how an assessment leads to a set of concrete objectives for intervention	❏	❏	❏
Describe the importance of reflective practice and supervision	❏	❏	❏
Identify in partnership with clients the appropriate model and method of intervention that best meets their needs	❏	❏	❏

Chapter 6: Effectiveness and evaluation

	Not at all	Partly	Very well
I can:			
Explain why practice should be evidence based	❏	❏	❏
Identify methods of practice evaluation	❏	❏	❏
Involve clients in evaluation using a children's rights perspective	❏	❏	❏
Explain how evaluation can contribute to the effective planning and management of CAMHS at both practice and agency levels	❏	❏	❏

Using this workbook

The exposition in the main body of the text will draw on a variety of sources, including government policy and practice guidance, social and health care theory and research findings.

The activities you will be asked to complete are designed to help you recognise and understand aspects of practice which you might not previously have known about or considered, and will help you to develop self-awareness by inviting you to relate your experience to the issues being explored. The temptation is to skip the activities – try not to because they can be valuable in ways you might not anticipate at first sight. They give you the opportunity to bring your own experience into the learning process, but also your responses will build up into a resource which you can draw on in current practice contexts and future personal and professional development.

With this in mind, it is useful to keep a separate booklet in which to write your responses. Think of this as a form of Learning Journal, and record things such as experiences at work which seem to you to relate to specific activities you have completed from the workbook. This can provide useful practice material for future reference and revision.

To help in training situations, all the activities and tables have been reproduced in easily photocopiable form at the back of the book.

Chapter 1
Multi-disciplinary working

Learning objectives

- Explain the importance of multi-disciplinary working.

- Describe the obstacles to, and ways to achieve effective multi-disciplinary work.

- Describe how changing patterns of service delivery are influencing professional relationships.

- Work in partnership to identify and analyse potential problems and appropriate responses.

Introduction

Interprofessional or multi-disciplinary care are contemporary terms often used synonymously to mean joint working between staff from different professional backgrounds. Staff may work in the same team location or operate from separate uni-professional teams. Within the same agency they may represent different disciplines or client groups. In whatever configuration joint working has always been recommended as the best way of delivering coherent and effective care in health and social work practice. Every social or health care textbook features injunctions for closer working between agencies, better communication, and clear lines of accountability.

Absence of these elements of practice is usually highlighted in all-too frequent inquiries into deaths involving child abuse, mental health, or social care situations. Government practice guidance emphasises these ideas in slick managerialist terms and appeals to systems-level co-ordination, enhanced procedures, and strategic planning. Translating these ideas into practice skills is more difficult than rhetorical slogans. In many situations you may be directly or indirectly involved in work in which your contribution, *however small*, could make a big difference to a successful outcome. In the context of child and adolescent mental health the role is pivotal in the following circumstances:

- In residential child care.

- As a classroom teacher or assistant.

- As child and family social workers.

- As convenors of inter-agency planning meetings.

- At case conferences involving child protection concerns.

- As a paediatric or community nurse.

- In long-term care planning and reviews.

- In a care management role.

- As contributors to multi-disciplinary intervention.

- In young offender teams.

- As referrers to specialist and community resources.

- In fostering and adoption contexts.

In whatever context of practice involving children and adolescents, you need to examine the complex web of agencies and staff available to contribute to the needs of a child or young person with mental health problems. This offers an opportunity to reflect on the potential for success, spot potential areas of professional disagreement or confusion, and clarify your particular contribution.

The challenges in working together

The range of staff involved in the delivery of child and adolescent mental health services is broad and the potential for disagreement, confusion or poor communication is high. The benefits of working together cannot be overstated but this should not happen at the expense of proper professional debate that sometimes can be difficult (Davis et al., 1997). However, before considering the diversity of professional and voluntary backgrounds engaged in this work, it is worth remembering that parents/carers provide over 90 per cent of the care of their children. They are the people who will be in most contact with the child or young person at the centre of concern. Therefore they must be seen as partners with whom an appropriate alliance is formed, even in the face of profound disagreements about the way forward.

Those parents socially excluded will have greater difficulty in promoting the mental health of their children, obtaining help if problems arise, and participating in the helping process (Audit Commission, 1998). The concept of partnership may be quite alien to some parents who will expect to be told what the matter with their child is and how it will be put right. Others will want to prescribe precisely what needs to happen. Making explicit and keeping in mind that partnership does not mean equal will help you and your client form a more effective relationship.

Working in multi-disciplinary contexts means addressing the different knowledge and value base of other staff, but it also means encountering a variety of views about service user participation and empowering strategies. Not all staff will be comfortable with notions of participatory practice and empowerment. The following list provides an indication of the potential reservoir of professional and voluntary resources available, several of whom may be involved with the same family at the same time:

- **Primary care:** based around GP practices and providing a child health service to enable, advise, and support parents. Offers diagnosis and access to help with mild and early signs of problems. Located within Primary Care Trust boundary.

- **Child health:** based in specialist units or clinics in acute or community settings. Paediatricians, health visitors, school nurses and other specialists involved in physical and developmental problems that include a mental health component.

- **Teachers:** based in schools with other support staff and educational psychologists in special units such as EBD schools. Offer early identification of learning difficulties, SEN and/or behavioural problems, and deliver personal and social skills education to promote mental health.

- **Social work and probation:** based around local authority structures and specialist units with children and family client group. Offer family support, child protection, and work with young offenders including identification of, and help with, mental health problems in co-operation with other agencies.

- **Voluntary sector:** based in family centres or peripatetic home visiting. A growing part of the mosaic of provision for children and young people where statutory services are inaccessible or inappropriate. Offer a preventive role, less stigma, and flexible response to local needs such as counselling, parent support, or advice and information.

- **Mental health specialists:** based in outpatient, inpatient, or specialist centres together with multi disciplinary staff such as social workers, psychotherapists, child and adolescent psychiatrists, psychologists, and family therapists. Offer assessment, management, and therapeutic interventions with individuals, groups or families.

Activity 1.1

a) Select a child or young person from your caseload. Write their name in the centre of a large piece of paper and then draw around them the professionals and other helping staff involved at some time in their care.

b) Now examine the staff involved and make a list of those who you feel close to and those who you do not. Explain the differences.

Changing patterns of service delivery

Research conducted over the past decade by diverse independent and government sources has found child and adolescent mental health services to be fragmented, under-resourced, poorly staffed, and ill-equipped to meet the needs of increasing numbers of troubled young people with a complex variety of mental health difficulties. The following set of principles for developing synchronised models of care to respond to identified need established a framework in which specialist CAMHS are advised to operate (Wallace et al., 1995):

- The majority of problems can be dealt with in primary care.

- Specialists should provide support to the other groups.

- The specialist service should be convenient and appropriate for children and adolescents.

- Specialist services should include both uni-disciplinary and multi-disciplinary resources to cover the spectrum of need.

- Specialist services should be targeted on categories of children with a high prevalence of mental health problems and should be distributed to provide maximum resources at points of need.

- There should be a co-ordinating structure, with shared strategies and policies, in order to reduce duplications, gaps and confusion for users.

- No uni-disciplinary service should work in isolation. Open channels of communication and procedures providing for ready access to other levels of the service should be agreed.

- Professional isolation should be avoided and professional accountability should be to individuals within the same discipline. This should not be confused with accountability for the provision of services.

- Services should be managed so that every profession shares in the organisation of intra-professional matters, such as audit, training, supervision, recruitment, and service development.

The organisational patterns for service delivery across all public services are now moving to multi-professional, multi-disciplinary and cross-departmental teams in order to reduce or eliminate delay. This is in effect, what is meant by government reference to cross-cutting approaches to the delivery of public services. In health and social care, this translates into multi-agency working and there are signs of new interprofessional teams being created. Ovretveit (1996) argues that it is important to be able to distinguish the type of multidisciplinary team so that:

- Practitioners understand their role.

- Managers can make changes to improve service quality.

- Planners can decide which type is most suited to the needs of a client population.

- Researchers can contribute to knowledge about which type is most effective.

Joint practitioner teams in health and social services can be described in three broad ways. The first refers to the degree of integration or closeness of working between professions. One way of achieving integration is the development of a core training programme for all staff. This would cover a range of relevant subjects for example:

- child and adolescent mental health

- assessment

- attachment theory

- emotional impact of divorce and separation

- therapeutic intervention

- child protection

- child development

- domestic violence

- resilient children

- preventive work

- bereavement and loss

- parenting skills

- anti-discriminatory practice

- Human Rights Act

- children's rights

Apart from increasing the knowledge and skills base of individual practitioners who come with different levels of prior training and staff development, the delivery mode of the training would not be profession-specific and thus unlike much conventional training. It would also be delivered not just to whole teams but to the whole CAMH service. The additional benefit of such a system-wide training programme would be closer integration within teams and across the local service. This concept is already manifesting to some extent with the example of the joint practitioner in learning disability, with original qualification in, for example, nursing and social work (Davis et al., 1999). Also, the new joint commissioning environment in health and social care enshrined in the Health Act (DoH, 1999) enables new services to be created where multi-disciplinary working is enhanced.

The second way of describing joint practitioner teams refers to the extent to which the team manages its resources as a collective and permanent presence, or as separate professional services. One of the vexed questions about effectiveness in the organisation of interprofessional care is how to mitigate the impact of the structural inhibitors thwarting attempts to cut across professional boundaries. These can be exemplified by the variety of geographical boundaries covered by health, social services and education authorities, combined with different pay scales and terms of employment (Young and Haynes, 1993; Leathard, 1994). In child and adolescent mental health services the Education, Health and Social Work structural hierarchies have traditionally militated against collaboration; preserved separate professional role identities; and inhibited interprofessional working (Fagin, 1992; Rawson, 1994; DfEE, 1998).

This has thwarted repeated attempts to achieve the much-vaunted seamless service for children and families in difficulties, as recommended in the Children Act (DoH, 1989). This problem can be overcome at the planning stage by providing each local service with a specific geographical catchment area based on the Primary Care Trust boundaries. This enables creative innovative thinking to flourish within and between agencies.

The third way of describing joint practitioner teams refers to how the team is led and how its members are managed. Team management is a potentially controversial subject where the challenge in multidisciplinary teams is to establish a structure that allows appropriate autonomy for practitioners from different professions but permits the team manager to control the use of staff time (Onyet et al., 1994). The professional background of such a manager will invariably cause concerns about favouritism or bias towards those from a similar background. Old rivalries and jealousies could quickly surface and threaten team harmony and collaborative working.

The job of manager therefore calls for highly developed diplomatic skills internally and externally, in relation to other agencies. Generally, there needs to be information cascade within the CAMHS tiered structure and outside into the broader children and families services framework. This is necessary to ensure more fluid communication between agencies in order to ensure as far as possible that the right service is supporting the right families at the right time. Within a focused CAMHS strategy, it is a crucial management task to liaise with other services providers in efforts to achieve the following:

- To streamline the referral processes between each service.

- To exchange referrals and share in consultation.

- To avoid families or referrers feeling passed around the system.

- To maintain service accountability.

- To monitor service eligibility criteria.

The multi-disciplinary nature of CAMH services offering intensive input, advice, information, parental guidance, and direct work with children in their own homes, or in preferred contexts such as schools, is indicative of a non-stigmatising acceptable service. The issue of roles and boundaries between different professionals has long been debated in the literature on health and social care and there is evidence that change is happening (Munley et al., 1982; NISW, 1982). For example the contemporary mode for joined up working and interprofessional care has promoted joint training and qualifications in working with people with learning disabilities and adults with mental health problems.

Recent initiatives to expand the role of nurses and social workers contribute to a blurring of roles often approved by clients (Snelgrove and Hughes, 2000; Williams et al., 1999; Pearce, 1999).

The stigma of child and adolescent mental health deters many young people from gaining access to the right help at the right time. This, combined with the profound feelings of guilt experienced by some parents which prevents them seeking support, means there is enormous unmet need in the community. Initiatives to bring together different professionals in offering a more accessible, appropriate, and acceptable service for troubled young people and their families is required to respond to a growing problem. Early intervention over a short period of time, with an eclectic mix of staff offering practical, therapeutic, activity based help and advice, is one viable part of an overall strategy.

Activity 1.2

a)   Obtain a copy of your local CAMHS strategy document.

b)   Discuss this with your line manager or supervisor and clarify your role in relation to it and your agency's responsibilities.

Overcoming the hurdles to implementation

Despite understanding the challenges to multi-disciplinary working and having a better organisational framework there are still hurdles to overcome in order to implement working together principles. While there is evidence of the positive benefits of skill mix and sharing knowledge thus leading to a blurring of former professional identities, there is other evidence that paradoxically, the encouragement of generic interprofessional working actually *reinforces* boundaries between professions (Brown et al., 2000). It is possible that as staff continue to train together, develop generic working and eventually harmonise status and pay differentials, there may be some resistance to relinquishing former roles, and there may even be a *strengthening* of the boundaries between professions. The challenge for the managers will be to preserve the distinctive individual professional expertise base, but not at the expense of service coherence. The challenge for practitioners will be to maintain a sense of loyalty to an identity while at the same time enabling that identity to change. Table 1.1 provides an illustration of the areas for consideration when planning multi-disciplinary care for a child.

Table 1.1: Areas for consideration when planning multi-disciplinary care

Initial discussion	Identify core group staff	Collate contributions to plan	Specify meeting dates	Clarify responsibility boundaries	Clarify assessment depth
The core group	Purpose and function	Methods to promote participatory practice	Anticipate potential inter-agency problems	Agree protocols for more attendees	Management of meeting-minutes, feedback
The plan	Overall aim	Timescale to implement	Methods to engage child and family	Agree procedures for changes to plan	Evaluation and plan monitoring
The key worker	Co-ordination	Direct work with child or family	Keeping an overview	Clarify joint working tasks	Manage inter-agency problems
The review	The remit of the review	Delegation of core group decisions	Guidance on reporting to the review	Enabling contributions from child and family	Providing support to staff

After Horwath and Calder, 1998.

The profile of social and health care teams working in child and adolescent mental health services largely reflects the professional white female population. There is some evidence that more male staff may help some boys and young men to engage more effectively with service provision. Clearly there is a dilemma in trying to achieve balanced interprofessional team membership with the need to maintain appropriate levels of expertise. This is not a problem unique to child and adolescent mental health services, but there is ample evidence that these factors weigh heavily when attempting to engage children and families already suffering under the pressure of racism and/or discrimination (Bhui and Olajide, 1999). It is important that children, families and carers have maximum choice when engaging with services aiming to meet their needs, and as discussed in Chapter 3, as important not to assume that black families only require black staff.

The practical results of efforts to encourage multi-disciplinary working aiming to improve the quality, delivery and co-ordination of all services for children and young people, need to be rigorously evaluated (DoH, 1998; Tucker et al., 1999; Rodney, 2000). In the history of child and adolescent mental health services there has always been a recognition that multi-disciplinary effort needs to be brought to bear on the difficulties of troubled children. That model has now been updated with initiatives such as, for example, Family Support Teams functioning to fulfil a multi-disciplinary role within a CAMHS struggling to cope with increased demand (Walker, 2001).

This model could be the genesis for a new primary mental health care professional, within a preventive configuration, with implications for training, qualifications, accreditation, and employment which demonstrably reflects an interprofessional perspective. They would be the embodiment of multi-disciplinary working and an attractive prospect for practitioners keen to use helping skills in direct work. The concept of early intervention is critical in child and adolescent mental health because there are few opportunities to make an impact in the developmental windows of opportunity that present in young people, before problems become entrenched. Primary mental health care staff intervening successfully at the appropriate moment could reduce vulnerability to later mental health problems in adulthood, with all the social, interpersonal, and economic savings for those individuals, their families, and society.

Primary mental health care practitioners are already beginning to be appointed within CAMHS and could eventually be the professional glue to hold the four-tier structure together. Working to bridge the gap between primary care and specialist care in child and adolescent mental health services they come from a multi-disciplinary range of professional backgrounds and are positioning themselves to strengthen and support CAMHS provision by a variety of means:

- Early recognition and intervention in CAMH problems.
- Helping other staff make informed decisions about potential referrals.
- Joint working in assessment of needs.
- Supporting teachers with consultancy and advice.
- Offering education and training to primary care staff.
- Working directly with children and young people or parent/carers.
- Consolidating primary care staff skills in identification and management of CAMH issues.
- Providing an effective gateway to specialist support or SEN assessment.

Activity 1.3

a) **In partnership with a colleague from another agency select a closed case you were both previously engaged with.**

b) **Review and reflect on the process of multi-disciplinary working, highlighting where things went wrong, where things went well, and why.**

Partnership and interprofessional relationships

The increased use of voluntary agencies and unqualified family support staff is one facet of the CAMHS strategy to provide more people to help parents quickly, rather than placing them on long waiting lists for specialist help, while their children's behaviour deteriorates. These staff require adequate training, supervision and support. Effort put in to improving relationships between staff can benefit them and their clients. The limited knowledge base of some staff may prevent them assessing accurately and lead them to interpret a child's behaviour as wilful rather than a reaction to adverse circumstances, for example. The evidence suggests in essence, bringing services closer to the children and families requiring them. At the same time it is important to make sure that there is a good fit between the expertise of the staff involved and the complexity of the problem (Durlak and Wells, 1997; Davis et al., 1997; Ouellette et al., 1999; Dulmus and Rapp-Paglicci, 2000).

This means more integrated provision at the primary or Tier One level, with multi-disciplinary staff receiving training and support to intervene in ways that meet the needs of the local community. In addition a community work dimension is required to energise and mobilise the latent strengths of individuals and groups who can act as grassroots facilitators to help create preventive resources when and where they are needed. Such an organisational model requires a systems-level method of evaluation in order to test its effectiveness in delivering better outcomes for children and young people. A system of care made up of multiple agencies working together acknowledges that troubled children have multiple needs which require, at different times, different combinations of a broad range of health and social care agencies.

However, there is some evidence that just altering the service delivery configuration of child and adolescent mental health services will not, of itself, translate into improved outcomes for troubled children (Morrissey et al., 1997). The focus of research needs to embrace evaluation of both the organisational, and the therapeutic, impact, and how these two variables interact. The strain imposed on professional relationships can impact adversely on relationships with service users. The increasing demands for service provision are producing pressure to spread staff thinly across a range of need even though this may not, in the long run prevent the mental health of some children and young people deteriorating, and only scratch the surface of other more serious problems. Your task is to research the local community to identify naturally occurring resources/networks of people, who with support and encouragement can bring their expertise to the search for solutions.

There is growing interest in the further development of interprofessional and multi-disciplinary working in order to maximise the effectiveness of interventions to meet the diverse needs of multi-cultural societies and service users (Magrab et al., 1997; Oberheumer, 1998; Tucker et al., 1999). The evidence suggests there are cost-benefit advantages if duplication of tasks can be avoided, relationships between staff are improved and there is more opportunity to maintain the child at the centre of attention rather than the needs of the various organisations. It has been estimated for example, that between the ages of 10 and 28, young people with a conduct disorder each cost over £100,000 more in services used than those without a conduct disorder (Knapp and Scott, 1998). The suggestion is that rather than passing the young person round the system of costly service provision for repeated assessments, it would be preferable to sustain work over a *consistent* period with as few staff that need to be involved.

The terminology employed by staff in key agencies is one of the factors militating against more effective multi-disciplinary work as noted in Chapter 2. Health professionals tend to talk about mental health problems and psychiatric disorders. Education staff talk about children who are presenting challenging behaviour, emotional or behavioural problems, or who have special educational needs. Social workers talk about children in need, at risk, suffering significant harm or some of the above. All these terms are used to describe children with broadly similar problems. A boy can be described by a psychiatrist as having a conduct disorder, while a teacher might say he is aggressive and attention seeking, while a social worker might describe the same boy as emotionally neglected.

The characteristics of successful multi-disciplinary work occur within a framework familiar to you. It begins with assessment then proceeds through decision-making, planning, monitoring, evaluation, and finally to closure. It is argued that this common framework employed by most health and social care staff, offers the optimum model for encouraging reflective practice to be at the core of contemporary child and adolescent mental health work (Taylor and White, 2000). Each agency involved can measure effectiveness against this basic framework and find common ground on which to consider the best way of helping a troubled child or adolescent by:

- Examining the impact of the intervention in meeting the child's needs.

- Evaluating staff inputs and strategies.

- Auditing organisational demands and resources against objectives and priorities.

Reflective practice in work with child and adolescent mental health problems offers the opportunity to shift beyond functional analysis to making active links between the value base, policy-making process, and the variety of interventions conducted. Combined with this practice-led motivation for multi-disciplinary working, there is evidence that government policy imperatives requiring closer co-operation between professionals coming into contact with children and families are having an effect (Eber et al., 1996; Vandenberg and Grealish, 1996; Sutton, 2000). Your skills in relationship-building, combined with your ability to network and share information, make you ideally suited to advance this agenda.

The aim is for a seamless web of provision from primary through to tertiary care where needs are recognised, assessed and interventions formulated on a preventive basis in order to stop small, manageable difficulties developing into big intractable problems. Without such early intervention within a holistic multi-factoral approach, children suffering early difficulties run the risk of becoming troubled adults with all the greater social, psychological and financial consequences that entails (Bayley, 1998). Your work is central to the success of this project provided you can construct a distinctive capacity for facilitating multi-agency co-operation.

Activity 1.4

a) **Make contact with a different practitioner from another agency involved in your local CAMHS.**

b) **Together, draw up an action plan of how to improve inter-agency communication and review this in 3 months.**

■ LEARNING REVIEW

In this chapter we have tackled the issue of multi-disciplinary working and examined some of the potential areas for enhancing communication and working practices. The importance of multi-disciplinary working has been explained in terms of government policy expectations and better outcomes for children and adolescents. We have noted the large number of potential participants in this area of work all of whom will have distinctive skills, knowledge and perceptions of child and adolescent mental health problems.

The concept of working together and in partnership has been extended to include not just interprofessional relationships but also the preferred mode with children and families. Some of these families will be unfamiliar with and traditionally hard to engage in the helping process. We have reviewed some of the characteristics and strategies for helping overcome hurdles to enhanced co-operation between practitioners and clients.

Multi-disciplinary and interprofessional teams involved in the delivery of CAMHS are developing under new policy and practice arrangements. The need for joint education and training is paramount if the aim of intervening early to prevent emerging mental health problems from growing into larger ones is to be achieved, and to direct the most appropriate and effective intervention to those that have become established. The initiative is now with practitioners to make practical plans to improve inter-agency co-operation.

References and further reading

Audit Commission (1998) *Child and Adolescent Mental Health Services*. London, HMSO.

Bayley R (1998) *Transforming Children's Lives: The Importance of Early Intervention*. London, Family Policy Studies Centre.

Bhui K and Olajide D (1999) *Mental Health Service Provision for a Multi-Cultural Society*. London, Saunders.

Brown B, Crawford P and Darongkamas J (2000) Blurred Roles and Permeable Boundaries: The Experience of Multidisciplinary Working in Community Mental Health. *Health and Social Care in The Community*. 8: 6, 425-35.

Davis H et al. (1997) A Description and Evaluation of a Community Child Mental Health Service. *Clinical Child Psychology and Psychiatry*. 2: 2, 221-38.

Davis J, Rendell P and and Sims D (1999) The Joint Practitioner: A New Concept in Professional Training. *Journal of Interprofessional Care*.13: 4, 395-404.

DfEE (1998) *Towards an Interdisciplinary Framework for Developing Work With Children and Young People*. Childhood Studies Discipline Network. Conference Presentation: Cambridge, Robinson College.

DoH (1989) *The Children Act*. London, HMSO.

DoH (1998) *Modernising Mental Health Services: Safe, Supportive and Sensible*. London, HMSO.

DoH (1999) *The Health Act*. London, HMSO.

Dulmus C and Rapp-Paglicci L (2000) The Prevention of Mental Disorders in Children and Adolescents: Future Research and Public Policy Recommendations. *Families in Society: The Journal of Contemporary Human Services.* 81: 3, 294-303.

Durlak J and Wells A (1997) Primary Prevention Mental Health Programs for Children and Adolescents: A Meta-Analytic Review. *American Journal of Community Psychology.* 25: 2, 115-52.

Eber L, Osuch R and Redditt C (1996) School-Based Applications of the Wraparound Process: Early Results on Service Provision and Student Outcomes. *Journal of Child and Family Studies.* 5: 83-99.

Fagin C M (1992) Collaboration Between Nurses and Physicians: No Longer a Choice. *Academic Medicine.* 67: 5, 295-303.

Horwath J and Calder M (1998) Working Together to Protect Children on the Child Protection Register: Myth or Reality. *British Journal of Social Work.* 28: 879-95.

Knapp M and Scott S (1998) *Lifetime Costs of Conduct Disorder.* London, Mind Publications.

Leathard A (1994) *Going Inter-Professional.* London. Routledge.

Magrab P, Evans P and Hurrell P (1997) Integrated Services for Children and Youth at Risk: an International Study of Multidisciplinary Training. *Journal of Interprofessional Care.* 11: 1, 99-108.

Morrissey J, Johnsen M and Calloway M (1997) Evaluating Performance and Change in Mental Health Systems Serving Children and Youth: An Interorganizational Network Approach. *The Journal of Mental Health Administration.* 24: 1, 4-22.

Munley A, Powers C S and Williamson J B (1982) Humanising Nursing Home Environments: The Relevance of Hospice Principles. *International Journal of Ageing and Human Development.* 15: 263-84.

NISW (1982) *Social Workers: Their Role and Tasks.* London, NISW/Bedford Square Press.

Oberhuemer P (1998) A European Perspective on Early Years Training. In Abbott L and Pugh G (Eds.) *Training to Work in the Early Years: Developing The Climbing Frame.* Buckingham, Open University Press.

Onyet S, Heppleston T and Bushnell N (1994) *A National Survey of Community Mental Health Teams: Team Structure.* London, Sainsbury Centre for Mental Health.

Oullette P, Lazear K and Chambers K (1999) Action Leadership: The Development of an Approach to Leadership Enhancement for Grassroots Community Leaders in Children's Mental Health. *The Journal of Behavioural Health Services and Research.* 26: 2, 171-85.

Ovretveit J (1996) Five Ways to Describe a Multidisciplinary Team. *Journal of Interprofessional Care.* 10: 2. 163-71.

Pearce J (1999) Collaboration Between the NHS and Social Services in the Provision of Child and Adolescent Mental Health Services: A Personal View. *Child Psychology and Psychiatry Review.* 4: 4, 150-3.

Rawson D (1994) Models of Interprofessional Work: Likely Theories and Possibilities. In Leathard A (Ed.) *Going Interprofessional: Working Together for Health and Welfare.* London, Routledge.

Rodney C (2000) Pathways: A Model Service Delivery System. In Singh N, Leung J P and Singh A N *International Perspectives on Child and Adolescent Mental Health.* London, Elsevier.

Snelgrove S and Hughes D (2000) Interprofessional Relations Between Doctors and Nurses: Perspectives From South Wales. *Journal of Advanced Nursing.* 31: 3, 661-7.

Sutton C (2000) *Child and Adolescent Behaviour Problems.* Leicester, BPS.

Taylor C and White S (2000) *Practising Reflexivity in Health and Welfare.* Buckingham, Open University Press.

Tucker S et al. (1999) Developing an Interdisciplinary Framework for The Education and Training of Those Working With Children and Young People. *Journal of Interprofessional Care.* 13: 3, 261-70.

Vandenberg J and Grealish M (1996) Individualized Services and Supports Through the Wraparound Process: Philosophy and Procedures. *Journal of Child and Family Studies.* 5: 7-21.

Walker S (2001) Developing Child and Adolescent Mental Health Services. *Journal of Child Health Care.* 5: 2, 71-6.

Wallace S et al. (1995) *Epidemiologically Based Needs Assessment: Child and Adolescent Mental Health.* Wessex Institute of Public Health.

Williams B et al. (1999) Exploring Person Centredness: User Perspectives on a Model of Social Psychiatry. *Health and Social Care in The Community.* 7: 6, 475-82.

Young K and Haynes R (1993) Assessing Population Needs in Primary Health Care: The Problem of GOP Attachments. *Journal of Interprofessional Care.* 7: 1, 15-27.

Chapter 2
Definitions, prevalence and assessment

Learning objectives

- Describe the differences between mental health, mental health problem, and mental disorder.

- Explain the importance of theories of human growth and development.

- Describe risk and resilience factors in children and young people.

- Understand how knowledge, skills and values are integrated in effective assessment.

Introduction

Recent evidence indicates that 10 per cent of children up to the age of 18 years in Britain have a diagnosable mental health disorder. Higher rates exist among those living in inner city environments. One in five children and adolescents has a mental health problem which although less serious still requires professional support (Audit Commission, 1998; Office for National Statistics, 2001). It has been further estimated that child and adolescent mental health services are only reaching a minority of the population in their catchment areas requiring help. This indicates a large number of children and young people who are not receiving the necessary support and help to relieve their suffering.

The World Health Organisation estimates that one in five of the world's youth under 15 years of age suffer from mild to severe mental health disorders and that a large number of these children remain untreated as services to help them simply do not exist (WHO, 2001). This international context is important because within the overall figure there are significant similarities in the characteristics of problems but also differences in the prevalence rates. There is evidence to support the notion that cultural variations affect the prevalence rates, as well as figures showing consistently, for example, that boys have increased rates of externalising problems (aggression, delinquency) and that girls have increased rates of internalising problems (depression, anxiety, self-harm) (Dogra et al., 2002).

These findings are useful to consider when trying to understand the similarities and differences in children and young people's mental health in a diverse multi-ethnic society. Chapter 3 examines the evidence to contribute towards culturally competent practice in child and adolescent mental health, but for now the focus will be on the general ways in which the mental health of young people is conceptualised. The way in which psychiatry influences this agenda and some of the theoretical resources available to help you in your practice will also be examined.

Definitions and distinctions

Mental health problems are abnormalities of emotions, behaviour, or social relationships sufficiently marked or prolonged to cause suffering or risk to optimal development in the child or distress or disturbance in the family or community.

(Kurtz, 1992)

This formulation has echoes of the concept of child abuse to practitioners familiar with the Children Act definition and the concept of significant harm. Note the idea of abnormality of emotions and the notion of them being sufficiently marked or prolonged. This parallel is useful in as much as it reveals how imprecise these definitions are and how open they are to interpretation. Who decides what is abnormal, the worker, parent, or child? How is the notion of sufficiently marked or prolonged measured and against what standard?

Mental health is described as:

   ...a relative state of mind in which a person...is able to cope with, and adjust to, the recurrent stress of everyday living.

(Anderson and Anderson, 1995)

This definition of mental health introduces the idea of relativity and seems to advance the notion of coping with and adjusting to everyday living. Do black children and young people have to cope with and adjust to the everyday stress of racism? Can mental health be achieved by tolerating unemployment, poor housing, or social exclusion? Practitioners working in a psycho-social context will be attuned to the social dimension affecting children's mental health. You need to consider how you define the terms mental disorder and mental health and whether your practice aims to help children and young people 'adjust to the stress of everyday living' or challenge those stresses within a personal helping relationship. It is useful to the discussion about definitions and distinctions to make a distinction between mental health problems, and mental health disorders:

> *Problems are defined as a disturbance of function in one area of relationships, mood, behaviour, or development of sufficient severity to require professional intervention. Mental health disorders are defined as either a severe problem, commonly persistent, or the co-occurrence of a number of problems, usually in the presence of a number of risk factors.*
>
> (Wallace et al., 1995)

If it is problematic to define mental illness or disorder, then it is equally difficult to define what is meant by mental health for children and young people. It can mean different things to families, children, or professionals, and staff from different professional backgrounds might not share the same perception of what mental health is. A multi-disciplinary group (HAS, 1995) agreed that mental health in childhood and adolescence is indicated by:

- *A capacity to enter into and sustain mutually satisfying personal relationships.*

- *A continuing progression of psychological development.*

- *An ability to play and to learn so that attainments are appropriate for age and intellectual level.*

- *A developing moral sense of right and wrong.*

- *The degree of psychological distress and maladaptive behaviour being within normal limits for the child's age and context.*

It is important to try to understand the emotional world of children and young people if assessment and intervention strategies are going to meet their needs. The vocabulary, the perceptions, and the culture of emotional and behavioural difficulties that children and young people employ, need to be incorporated into the education, training and development of practitioners and other staff engaged in this work. A psychosocial perspective offers a holistic tool with which you can assemble all the important information about a child or young person that incorporates her or his internal as well as external context. Values and principles of empowerment are at the heart of good practice in child and adolescent mental health assessment.

Prevalence and problems

The research shows that one in 17 adolescents have harmed themselves – representing 200,000 11-15 year-olds. At the other end of the age spectrum there are increasing numbers of children under seven years of age being excluded from school due to uncontrollable behavioural problems. The increased rate of suicide over the last twenty eight years in children and adolescents is a cause of increasing concern and a stark indicator of the mental health of young people (McClure, 2001). Table 2.1 shows the prevalence and range of specific problems affecting children at different ages, and those indicating a gender bias.

Table 2.1: Prevalence of specific child and adolescent mental health problems

Emotional disorders	4.5-9.9% of 10 year olds
Major depression	0.5-2.5% of children, 2-8% of adolescents
Conduct disorders	6.2-10.8% of 10 year olds
Tic disorders	1-13% of boys, 1-11% of girls
Obsessive compulsive disorder	1.9% of adolescents
Hyperkinetic disorder (ADHD)	1 in 200 of all children
Encopresis (faecal soiling)	2.3% of boys, 0.7% of girls aged 7-8 years
Anorexia nervosa	0.5%-1% of 12-19 year olds
Bulimia nervosa	1% of adolescent girls and young women
Attempted suicide	2-4% of adolescents
Suicide	7.6 per 100,000 15-19 year olds
Alcohol abuse	29% of all 13 year olds drink weekly
Cannabis	3-5% of 11-16 year olds have used
Heroin and cocaine	Less than 1%
Hallucinogens	Increase reported

DoH, 1995

Factors associated with suicide in young people include depression, severe mental illness and personality disorder. Also, substance misuse, particularly alcohol, predates suicidal behaviour in many cases. The sharp increase in suicides among 15-to-19 year old men recently, mirrors the period which has shown a large increase in the use of alcohol and drugs among young people generally (Appleby et al., 1999). Disrupted relationships caused by family breakdown and social exclusion in terms of unemployment are factors strongly associated with young male suicide. There is an assumption that the gender disparity in rates of suicide in young people (three males to one female) reflects the changing roles of men and women in contemporary society.

This then leaves young women with higher levels of self-esteem and better coping strategies, and young men with a problematic masculine identity and an inability to acknowledge and communicate emotional difficulties (Gunnell et al., 1999). On the other hand there is evidence that changes to gender roles are having an effect on young women's capacity for externalising mental health problems with anti-social behaviour, rather than the traditional internalising of mental health problems. Between 2001 and 2002 there was a 40 per cent increase in the number of young women sentenced to secure custody (Youth Justice Board, 2002).

Recent evidence confirms for example that suicide is of particular concern in marginalised and victimised adolescent groups including gay, lesbian, and bisexual youth. Research suggests that despite the rhetoric of anti-discriminatory policies and professional statements of equality, heterosexist and homophobic attitudes continue to be displayed by some practitioners (Morrison and L'Heureux, 2001). This can further reinforce feelings of rejection, confusion and despair in troubled young people. Other evidence warns against a narrow definition of sexual-minority adolescents that pathologises their behaviour or wrongly assumes a higher risk of self-harming behaviour (Savin-Williams, 2001).

Poverty is one factor strongly associated with child mental health problems. The prevalence for any mental disorder ranges from 16 per cent among children living in families with a gross weekly household income of under £100, to nine per cent among children of families in the £300-£399 weekly income range. Only about six per cent of children and young people in those families earning £500 per week or more will suffer a mental health problem (ONS, 2001). Using this data it has been calculated that in a Primary School of 250 pupils there will be three children who are seriously depressed, 11 children suffering significant distress, 12 children who have phobias, and 15 children with a conduct disorder. In a typical Secondary School with 1000 pupils there will be 50 who are seriously depressed, 100 who are suffering significant distress, and 5-10 girls with an eating disorder. Many of these children will be exhibiting defensive behaviour such as aggression, poor attention, and disruption in the classroom, combined with poor attendance. They will almost certainly be seen as troublesome rather than suffering from a mental health problem thereby missing appropriate help and support.

Studies have shown that problems that begin in early childhood and remain untreated are likely to persist into later childhood and young adulthood. Parents and carers tend to assume that children will grow out of difficult behaviours and ascribe them to commonly held beliefs about normality. Phrases such as the terrible twos, childhood tantrums or adolescent turmoil enter common *parlance* and with them an unspoken assumption that these are somehow developmental milestones of a transient nature. The evidence, however, suggests that with conduct disorders (see below) and ADHD it is difficult to prevent the development of later anti-social activity. On the other hand, children with emotional disorders (see below) tend to be more successfully helped (Sutton, 2000). These are some of the more common disorders of mental health found in children and adolescents:

- **emotional disorders** (phobias, anxiety states, depression)

- **conduct disorders** (stealing, defiance, fire-setting, aggression, anti-social behaviour)

- **hyperkinetic disorders** (disturbance of activity and attention, ADHD)

- **developmental disorders** (autism, speech delay, poor bladder control)

- **eating disorders** (infant eating problems, anorexia nervosa, bulimia)

- **habit disorders** (tics, sleeping problems, soiling)

- **somatic disorders** (chronic fatigue syndrome)

- **psychotic disorders** (schizophrenia, manic depression, drug-induced psychoses)

Activity 2.1

a) **Consult with your friends, neighbours, relatives and partner about their perceptions of the behaviour and emotional world of children and young people these days.**

b) **Now consider these impressions with the data on prevalence and causation and explain the differences.**

Developmental theories

Recent advances in genetic research and refinement of developmental instruments for assessing children and young people's emotional and behavioural health have concluded that to regard nature and nurture as separate and independent is an oversimplification. The answer to what shapes children and adolescent's mental health is both nature and the environment, or rather, the interplay between the two. Whether the ideas of Freud, Klein, Piaget, Eriksen, Skinner, or Bowlby and others appeal to you, the important point is that it permits the adoption of some intellectual rigour to the way your work is organised (Mills and Duck, 2000; Beckett, 2002).

This can provide a framework within which the selection of assessment and intervention methods and models can take place. Crucially, it will enable a more systematic process to proceed in a recognisable direction or provide a knowledge base to discuss ideas put forward by other staff. This will be helpful in case conferences, legal proceedings, or report writing contexts. Sometimes it is helpful to acknowledge that there is no clear-cut explanation, or there are multiple interpretations for a child's emotional and behavioural problems that are concerning others.

Practitioners with a psycho-social perspective can especially utilise theoretical concepts from social policy and sociology to add to their framework of explanation. The combination can be powerful, adding weight to professional arguments and provide authority for interpretations. They can also be burdensome and confusing and should therefore always be used cautiously. They enable a social model of mental health to be acknowledged alongside others. The choice is again vast in the area of sociology alone. Marx, Durkheim, Mills, Parsons, Popper, or Habermas and others, offer a rich and diverse knowledge base (O'Donnell, 2002). The important point is the chosen theoretical preference can be identified and acknowledged, and a plan can proceed consistently within that premise.

The importance of reflective practice whilst undertaking work with children and adolescents cannot be emphasised enough. In the process of using measures of human growth and development it is crucial. This is because children and young people are constantly changing as are their circumstances. This requires a high level of concentration and alertness to changes that will be unique and unpredictable, as well as changes that appear to conform to a predictable developmental transition. Such changes may have nothing to do with your intervention and some may have everything to do with it. The key is in appreciating that developmental issues are significant and require you to have a good grasp of them (Thompson, 2002).

Summaries of the key elements of human growth and development as theoretical resources relevant to CAMHS are assembled below. They have been simplified to aid clarity and comparison and should be seen as part of a wide spectrum of potential, rather than deterministic, interactive causative factors in the genesis of child and adolescent mental health problems. Some social psychologists criticise the emphasis in child development theories on normative concepts and suggest enhancing the judging, measuring approach towards one that embodies context, culture, and competencies (Woodhead, 1998). The following summaries should be adapted to every individual situation encountered and always considered against the white, Eurocentric perceptions they embodied when first constructed.

Eriksen's psycho-social stages of development

Five of Eriksen's eight stages of development will be considered.

Year one: The infant requires consistent and stable care in order to develop feelings of security. Begins to trust the environment but can also develop suspicion and insecurity.

Deprivation at this stage can lead to emotional detachment throughout life and difficulties forming relationships.

Years 2-3: The child begins to explore and seeks some independence from parents/carers. A sense of autonomy develops but improved self-esteem can combine with feelings of shame and self-doubt. Failure to integrate this stage may lead to difficulties in social integration.

Years 4-5: The child needs to explore the wider environment and plan new activities. Begins to initiate activities but fears punishment and guilt as a consequence. Successful integration results in a confident person, but problems can produce deep insecurities.

Years 6-11: The older child begins to acquire knowledge and skills to adapt to surroundings. Develops sense of achievement but marred by possible feelings of inferiority and failure if efforts are denigrated.

Years 12-18: The individual enters stage of personal and vocational identity formation. Self-perception heightened, but potential for conflict, confusion, and strong emotions.

Freud's psychosexual stages of development

Year one: The oral stage during which the infant obtains its principal source of comfort from sucking the breast milk of the mother, and the gratification from the nutrition.

Years 2-3: The anal stage when the anus and defecation are the major sources of sensual pleasure. The child is preoccupied with body control with parental/carer encouragement. Obsessional behaviour and over-control later in childhood could indicate a problematic stage development.

Years 4-5: The phallic stage, with the penis the focus of attention is the characteristic of this psychosexual stage. In boys the oedipus complex and in girls the electra complex are generated in desires to have a sexual relationship with the opposite sex parent. The root of anxieties and neuroses can be found here if transition to the next stage is impeded.

Years 6-11: The latency stage, which is characterised by calm after the storm of the powerful emotions preceding it.

Years 12-18: The genital stage whereby the individual becomes interested in opposite-sex partners as a substitute for the opposite-sex parent, and as a way of resolving the tensions inherent in oedipul and electra complexes.

Bowlby's attachment theory

The following scheme represents the process of healthy attachment formation. Mental health problems may develop if an interruption occurs in this process, if care is inconsistent, or if there is prolonged separation from main carer.

Months 0-2: This stage is characterised by pre-attachment undiscriminating social responsiveness. The baby is interested in voices and faces and enjoys social interaction.

Months 3-6: The infant begins to develop discriminating social responses and experiments with attachments to different people. Familiar people elicit more response than strangers.

Months 7-36: Attachment to main carer is prominent with the child showing separation anxiety when carer is absent. The child actively initiates responses from the carer.

Years 3-18: The main carer's absences become longer, but the child develops a reciprocal attachment relationship. The child and developing young person begins to understand the carer's needs from a secure emotional base.

Piaget's stages of cognitive development

Years 0-1.5: The sensori-motor stage characterised by infants exploring their physicality and modifying reflexes until they can experiment with objects and builds a mental picture of things around them.

Years 1.5-7: The pre-operational stage when the child acquires language, makes pictures, and participates in imaginative play. The child tends to be self-centred and fixed in her/his thinking believing they are responsible for external events.

Years 7-12: The concrete operations stage when a child can understand and apply more abstract tasks such as sorting or measuring. This stage is characterised by less egocentric thinking and more relational thinking-differentiation between things. The complexity of the external world is beginning to be appreciated.

Years 12-18: The stage of formal operations characterised by the use of rules and problem-solving skills. The child moves into adolescence with increasing capacity to think abstractly and reflect on tasks in a deductive, logical way.

A more recent view of personality development lists five factors that combine elements of the older more classic ways of understanding a child or adolescent together with notions of peer acceptability and adult perceptions (Hampson, 1995; Jones and Jones, 1999):

- **Extroversion** – includes traits such as extroverted/introverted, talkative/quiet, bold/timid.

- **Agreeableness** – based on characteristics such as agreeable/disagreeable, kind/unkind, selfish/unselfish.

- **Conscientiousness** – reflects traits such as organised/disorganised, hardworking/lazy, reliable/unreliable, thorough/careless, practical/impractical.

- **Neuroticism** – based on traits such as stable/unstable, calm/angry, relaxed/tense, unemotional/emotional.

- **Openness to experience** – includes the concept of intelligence, together with level of sophistication, creativity, curiosity and cognitive style in problem-solving situations.

Activity 2.2

a) Review the information above on developmental theories and select the one or those that fit with your beliefs about the influences on people.

b) Now use it/them to construct your own personal developmental process and make an assessment of yourself at age 13.

Risk and resilience factors

The evidence suggests that interplay between characteristics in the child and their environment increase the risks of developing mental health problems. Practitioners ought to find this paradigm fits with a holistic psycho-social framework for assessment and intervention. Table 2.2 (overleaf) illustrates the risk factors commonly identified as indicators of potential child mental health problems.

The rise in drug and substance abuse, alcohol consumption and the widening gap between rich and poor all contribute to a fertile environment for risk factors to escalate (Townsend, 1993). The risks to children from parents with mental health problems are well understood, yet there is still evidence of a lack of liaison between adult and child and adolescent mental health services which would better serve all the family members (Howe, 1999; Parsloe, 1999; Hetherington and Baistow, 2001). Risk assessment in the context of child protection tends to focus on the likelihood of a parent harming a child in the future. This usually takes place after an incident has already occurred, with the aim of preventing a recurrence, or identifying those families where harm is likely to take place (Parsloe, 1999).

Preventive and predictive risk assessment aims to target support services early enough to reach those most in need. However, this process can be discriminatory, inaccurate, and statistically unreliable. Poor families and socially excluded people can feel persecuted (Dingwall, 1989). Checklists of predictive factors have led to the construction of characteristics of parents more likely to harm their children. They imply that it is only in socially disadvantaged families where abuse is more likely to take place, or that single parents, those abused in childhood, or fostered and adopted children are likely to abuse their own children. This is inaccurate, unhelpful and potentially dangerous (Parsloe, 1999).

Table 2.2: Factors that are known to increase the risk of mental health problems in children and young people

- **Child risk factors:**
  - genetic influences
  - low IQ and learning disability
  - specific developmental delay
  - communication difficulty
  - difficult temperament
  - physical illness, especially if chronic and/or neurological
  - academic failure
  - low self-esteem

- **Family risk situations:**
  - overt parental conflict
  - family breakdown
  - inconsistent or unclear discipline
  - hostile and rejecting relationships
  - failure to adapt to a child's changing developmental needs
  - abuse – physical, sexual or emotional
  - parental psychiatric illness
  - parental criminality, alcoholism, and personality disorder
  - death and loss – including loss of friendships

- **Environmental risk factors:**
  - socio-economic disadvantage
  - homelessness
  - disaster
  - discrimination
  - other significant life events

Audit Commission, 1998.

The tools of risk assessment tend not to take account of cultural factors in their construction or interpretation. There is considerable pressure on social workers and their managers to make safe decisions, which can be judged as such before and after the event. Such an impossible task leads to defensive practice and the neglect of child mental health problems, which are hard to quantify. Children with several identified risk factors demonstrate resilience and do not develop mental health problems. As well as understanding why some children develop mental health problems, it is crucially important to learn more about those who in similar circumstances do not.

Research is required to analyse the nature of these resilient children to understand whether coping strategies or skills can be transferred to other children. Positive factors such as reduced social isolation, good schooling, and supportive adults outside the family appear to help. These are the very factors missing in asylum seekers, refugees, and other ethnic minority families who live in deprived conditions and suffer more socio-economic disadvantages than other children do. Certain key factors appear to promote resilience in young people to mental health problems and disorders:

- self-esteem

- sociability and autonomy

- family compassion and warmth

- absence of parental discord

- social support systems

- encouragement of personal effort and coping

Mental health problems frequently present in children and young people who are causing concern to staff working in education, social services, or in youth justice contexts. The capability of teachers, social workers, and probation officers, and the capacity of the services within which they work to identify these mental health problems are crucial. Chapter 5 discusses in more detail how to improve interprofessional care in this area. Being able to respond in a timely and appropriate manner to the early signs of mental health problems, may make all the difference to the chance of effective intervention for the young person. There remain, however, barriers to the development of wider and better understanding of mental health difficulties among and between professionals in all agencies coming into contact with troubled children. These include:

- A widespread reluctance to 'label' a child or young person as mentally ill.

- A poor appreciation of what specialist child psychology and psychiatry services can do.

- The ways in which priorities are set within the statutory framework of the Mental Health Act 1983, Children Act 1989 and the Education Act 1993.

- Lack of knowledge and close working between agencies.

It has been established that a confluence of several risk factors in childhood can create the conditions for later psychosocial difficulty, including socio-economic disadvantage, child abuse, and parental mental illness. However, there are protective mechanisms that can mitigate the chance of some children going on to develop anti-social behaviour or serious mental health problems. A thorough assessment of risk *and* resilience factors is advocated (Rutter, 1985). These include the child's response to stress being determined by the capacity to appraise and attach meaning to their situation. Age-related susceptibilities that permit older children to use their greater understanding compared to younger children need to be understood.

How a child deals with adversity either actively or reactively, and the ability to act positively, is a function of self-esteem and feelings of self-efficacy rather than indicating any inherent problem-solving skills. Features as varied as secure stable affectionate relationships, success, achievement, and temperamental attributes can foster such cognitive capacity. Rutter (ibid) concludes that protection does not lie in the buffering effects of some supportive factor. Rather, all the evidence points towards the importance of developmental links. The quality of a child's resilience to developing mental health problems or emotional and behavioural difficulties is influenced by early life experiences but is not determinative of later outcomes.

This highlights the importance of assessment methods that take account of not just individual characteristics within the child but equally within the family and broader environment. In combination these protective factors may create a chain of indirect links that foster escape from adversity. Organising services across the spectrum of multi-agency provision in partnership between CAMHS professionals and parents, offers the opportunity to bring out dormant protective factors to interrupt the causal chain of negative events (Little and Mount, 1999). A progressive, preventive environment that promotes children's emotional well-being is preferable to reacting to the consequences of neglect or abuse. Individual factors regarded as promoting resilience include:

- an even and adaptable temperament

- a capacity for problem-solving

- physical attractiveness

- a sense of humour

- good social skills and supportive peers

- a sense of autonomy and purpose

- secure attachment to at least one parent

- links with the wider community

Activity 2.3

a) Using details of a child or young person from your caseload write a list of three risk factors and three resilience factors.

b) Now weigh them up and decide whether the balance falls towards risk or resilience.

Multi-faceted assessment

The dimensions of child, family and environmental factors in the *Framework for Assessment of Children in Need* are a useful tool in the process of multi-faceted assessment (DoH, 2000):

The dimensions of a child's developmental needs

- **Health** – growth, development, physical or mental well-being, genetic factors, disability, diet, exercise, immunisation, sex education, substance misuse.

- **Education** – play and interaction, books, skills, interests, achievements, school, special educational needs.

- **Emotional and behavioural development** – appropriateness of responses, expression of feelings, actions, attachment, temperament, adaptability, self-control, stress responses.

- **Identity** – self-perception, abilities, self-image, achievement, individuality, race, religion, age, gender, sexuality, disability, sense of belonging, acceptance.

- **Family and social relationships** – empathy, affectionate relationships, siblings, friendships.

- **Social presentation** – appearance, behaviour, understanding of social self, dress, cleanliness, personal hygiene, use of advice.

- **Self-care skills** – acquisition of competencies, independence, practical skills, confidence, problem solving, vulnerabilities, impact of disability.

The dimensions of parenting capacity

- **Basic care** – providing for physical needs, medical care, food, hygiene, warmth, shelter, clothing, hygiene.

- **Ensuring safety** – protecting child from abuse, harm or danger, unsafe adults, self harm, recognition of hazards.

- **Emotional warmth** – meeting emotional needs, racial and cultural identity, valued, secure, stable and affectionate relationships, responsive to child's needs, praise, warm regard, encouragement and physical comfort.

- **Stimulation** – cognitive stimulation, intellectual development, promoting social opportunities, interaction, communication, talking, encouraging questions, play, school attendance, enabling success.

- **Guidance and boundaries** – help guide emotions and behaviour, demonstrating and modelling behaviour and interactions with others, setting boundaries, moral development, and respect own values, anger management, consideration for others, discipline.

- **Stability** – maintains secure attachments, consistent emotional warmth, predictable responses, maintain contact with other family members and significant others.

The dimensions of family and environmental factors

- **Family history and functioning** – genetic and psycho-social factors, household composition, history of parent's own childhood, life events, family functioning, sibling relationships, parental strengths and difficulties, absent parents, separated parents relationship.

- **Wider family** – who does the child feel attached to? Related and non-related persons and wider family, role of relatives and friends, the importance of other people in family network.

- **Housing** – amenities, accessibility, sanitation, cooking facilities, sleeping arrangements, hygiene, and safety.

- **Employment** – who works, pattern of employment, meaning of work to child, impact of work or absence of work on child.

- **Income** – availability, sufficiency, welfare benefits, how resources are used, financial difficulties and the affect on child.

- **Family's social integration** – local neighbourhood, community, degree of integration or isolation, peer groups, friendships, social networks.

- **Community resources** – local facilities and resources, health care, day care, schools, places of worship, transport, shops, leisure activities, standard of resources.

The complex interplay across all three domains should be carefully understood and analysed. The interactions between different factors within the domains are not straightforward. It is important that you gather and record information accurately and systematically. Information should be checked and discussed with parents and children. Differences in perceptions about the information and its relative significance should be recorded. It is important you assess and understand the strengths and difficulties within families and relate these to the vulnerabilities and protective factors in the child's world. The impact of what is happening on the child should be clearly identified (DoH, 2000).

The literature on assessment in child and adolescent mental health and current Department of Health guidance are gradually improving to emphasise multi-faceted assessment. The emphasis is on the need for analysing and weighing the information generated during the assessment process ensuring this is underpinned by partnership practice. A number of themes emerge from the research literature that help to consider how to achieve this in the context of family and children's difficulties. These include the importance of multi-factorial causal explanations and the contribution of structural variables to childhood problems articulated by several authors (Sutton, 1999; Cole et al., 1995; Rutter et al., 1994). Understanding assessment as a process rather than a single event will help create the appropriate atmosphere with children and their carers, who require patience and a calm, measured stance from you.

Assessment is also thought of as a one-way process. It is something done by practitioners to others or it involves the gathering of information from those apparently familiar with the child or adolescent of concern. Your work can benefit from appreciating the interactive nature of the assessment process. In other words the very nature of assessment will affect that which is being assessed. Simply engaging with a child in some basic drawing or play activity to gain an understanding of them can begin to change the child's behaviour. Interpretation of the child's emotional and behavioural state therefore needs to take account of the potential impact of the assessment process.

The importance of variation in perception of children's behaviour depending on the theoretical model used, and the evidence on assessment methodology is crucial in determining the course and type of support offered. The interplay of these factors and the beneficial effects of developing a synthesis of models of intervention suggest precise targeted responses to particular children's difficulties combined with an expansive approach addressing social issues affecting children and families (Hill, 1999). The different way children's behaviour is understood by the child, the parent or carer and the professionals who encounter the child are important to acknowledge and incorporate in any care plan or supportive intervention. Differences in perception can therefore be seen as explanatory potential rather than implicitly conflictual.

Practitioners have the opportunity to employ communication and relationship skills in direct family support work which they traditionally find rewarding and which service users find more acceptable than intrusive, investigative risk assessment. Your role in multi-agency assessment and planning becomes significant in this context where several perceptions can be expressed, based on diverse evidence and different levels of professional anxiety. Practitioners managing these processes with individuals or groups in planning meetings, case conferences or case reviews require advanced negotiation and decision-making skills.

Activity 2.4

a) Together with a colleague, each write down three lists of your own characteristics at age 7 as you felt, as your parents saw you, and as your class teacher perceived you.

b) Note the similarities and differences, and think about and discuss together what concepts informed those differences.

■ LEARNING REVIEW

In this chapter we have considered some definitions of mental health problems and disorders as well as what might constitute mental health in children and adolescents. We have considered popular understanding of child and adolescent mental health problems against the statistical prevalence and how this affects parents or carers perceptions of their children.

We have thought about the risk factors in the development of mental health problems in young people and acknowledged the part played by poverty and early childhood adversity. A holistic and psycho-social framework for understanding the potential for mental health problems to develop has been highlighted as a useful starting point in the assessment process.

We have reviewed some of the classic developmental theories that are available to guide the assessment process and provide explanatory evidence for understanding troubled children and adolescents. These need to be adapted to ensure their relevance for our culturally diverse society.

Risk and resilience factors have been evaluated in order to enable practitioners to intervene early to prevent minor problems developing into major problems. The importance of trying to distinguish those children who in adverse circumstances manage to maintain their resilience has been emphasised.

Multi-faceted assessment requires the synthesis of a wide spectrum of data. The three dimensions of the framework for the assessment of children in need – child and parental capacity and family environment, when combined offer a comprehensive source of explanatory material and the ingredients for planning your intervention.

References and further reading

Anderson K and Anderson L (Eds.) (1995) *Mosbys Pocket Dictionary of Nursing, Professions Allied to Medicine.* London, Mosby.

Appleby L, Cooper J and Amos T (1999) Psychological Autopsy Study of Suicides by People Aged Under 35. *British Journal of Psychiatry.* 175: 168-74.

Audit Commission (1998) *Child and Adolescent Mental Health Services.* London, HMSO.

Beckett C (2002) *Human Growth and Development.* London, Sage.

Cole E, Leavey G and King M (1995) Pathways to Care for Patients With First Episode of Psychosis. A Comparison of Ethnic Groups. *British Journal of Psychiatry.* 167: 770-6.

Dingwall R (1989) Some Problems About Predicting Child Abuse and Neglect. In Stevenson O (Ed.) *Child Abuse: Public Policy and Professional Practice.* Hemel Hempstead, Harvester Wheatsheaf.

Dogra N, Parkin A, Gale F and Frake C (2002) *A Multidisciplinary Handbook of Child and Adolescent Mental Health for Front-Line Professionals.* London, Jessica Kingsley.

DoH (2001) *Framework for The Assessment of Children in Need.* London, HMSO.

Gunnell D, Wehner H and Frankel S (1999) Sex Differences in Suicide Trends in England and Wales. *The Lancet.* 353: 556-7.

Hampson S (1995) The Construction of Personality. In Hampson S E and Coleman A M (Eds.) *Individual Differences and Personality.* London, Longman.

Hetherington R and Baistow K (2001) Supporting Families With a Mentally Ill Parent: European Perspectives on Interagency Cooperation. *Child Abuse Review.* 10: 351-65.

Hill M (1999) *Effective Ways of Working With Children and Their Families.* London, Jessica Kingsley.

Howe G (1999) *Mental Health Assessments.* London, Jessica Kingsley.

Jones D and Jones M (1999) The Assessment of Children With Emotional and Behavioural Difficulties-Psychometrics and Beyond. In Cooper C (Ed.) *Understanding and Supporting Children With Emotional and Behavioural Difficulties.* London, Jessica Kingsley.

Kurtz Z (Ed.) (1992) *With Health in Mind Quality Review Series on Mental Health Care for Children and Young People.* London, Action for Sick Children/NW Thames RHA.

Little M and Mount K (1999) *Prevention and Early Intervention With Children in Need.* Aldershot, Ashgate.

McClure G (2001) Suicide in Children and Adolescents in England and Wales 1970-1998. *British Journal of Psychiatry.* 178: 469-74.

Mills R and Duck S (2000) *The Developmental Psychology of Personal Relationships.* Chichester, Wiley.

Morrison L and L'Heureux J (2001) Suicide and Gay/Lesbian/Bisexual Youth: Implications for Clinicians. *Journal of Adolescence.* 24: 39-49.

NHS Health Advisory Service (1995) *Together We Stand: Child and Adolescent Mental Health Services.* London, HMSO.

O'Donnell G (2002) *Mastering Sociology.* London, Palgrave.

Office for National Statistics (2001) *Child and Adolescent Mental Health.* London, HMSO.

Parsloe P (1999) (Ed.) *Risk Assessment in Social Care and Social Work.* London, Jessica Kingsley.

Rutter M (1985) Resilience in the Face of Adversity. *British Journal of Psychiatry.* 147: 598-611.

Rutter M, Hersov L and Taylor E (1994) *Child and Adolescent Psychiatry.* Oxford, Blackwell.

Savin-Williams R (2001) A Critique of Research on Sexual Minority Youth. *Journal of Adolescence.* 24: 5-13.

Sutton C (1999) *Helping Families With Troubled Children.* London, Wiley.

Sutton C (2000) *Child and Adolescent Behaviour Problems.* Leicester, BPS.

Thompson N (2002) *Building The Future: Social Work With Children, Young People and Their Families.* Lyme Regis, Russell House Publishing.

Townsend P (1993) *The International Analysis of Poverty.* Hemel Hempstead, Harvester Wheatsheaf.

Wallace S, Crown J, Cox A and Berger M (1995) *Epidemiologically Based Needs Assessment: Child and Adolescent Mental Health.* Wessex Institute of Public Health.

Woodhead M (1998) Understanding Child Development in the Context of Children's Rights. In Cunninghame C (Ed.) *Realising Children's Rights*. London, Save The Children.

World Health Organisation (2001) *World Health Day. Mental Health: Stop Exclusion Dare to Care*. Geneva, WHO.

Youth Justice Board (2002) *Building on Success: YJB Annual Review*. London, HMSO.

Chapter 3
Culturally competent practice

Learning objectives

- Describe what is meant by culturally competent practice.

- Illustrate the importance of cultural identity to the mental health of a diverse society.

- Explain how understanding of oppression and discrimination influences contemporary practice.

- Understand the mental health needs of black and ethnic minority families.

Introduction

The shifting population demographics of the United States of America indicate that ethnic minority children will become the majority of those under age eighteen within the next fifty years. In Britain, and in other European countries, in some areas ethnic minority families make up a greater proportion of the population while overall the population profile is ageing. Globalisation, European economic and political convergence, ethnic conflicts and the relaxation of boundaries between countries are enabling the displacement of asylum seeking and refugee families.

These factors, combined with the widening gap between rich and poor countries, are all contributing to the accelerating historical trends of migration and immigration leading to the widening and deepening of the multi-cultural tapestry of complex, modern, diverse Western societies. Research has highlighted the inequitable, oppressive, and poor quality services available for ethnic minority families in these societies (Cole et al., 1995; Bhui, 1997; Bhui and Olajide, 1999; Fernando, 2002). It is crucial therefore, that the organisation and training of all professionals working in child and adolescent mental health services is culturally competent. Table 3.1 illustrates the depth of cultural diversity recorded at the previous census.

Cultural competence has been defined as a set of congruent attitudes, behaviours, and policies that are part of an agency, system or professional group, and that enable these groups to work effectively in cross-cultural situations. For you to achieve competence you must be aware of your own culture, refrain from judging differences as necessarily deviant and understand the dynamics of working class cultures. You must develop a base of knowledge about your clients' culture, and adapt your skills to fit the child or young person's cultural context (Cross et al., 1989). Culture includes age-specific culture – a critical part of the context of trying to engage with disaffected young people and troubled children. The evidence suggests that peer-initiated interventions and supportive relationships have a significant impact on children and adolescents with mental health problems.

The Western model of illness regards the mind as distinct from the body and defines mental illness or mental health according to negative, deficit characteristics. In non-western cultures such as Chinese, Indian and African, mental health is often perceived as a harmonious balance between a person's internal and external influences. Thus a person is intrinsically linked to their environment and vice versa. The Western model of mental illness ignores the religious or spiritual aspects of the culture in which it is based. However, Eastern, African and Native American cultures tend to integrate them (Fernando, 2002). Spirituality and religion as topics in general do not feature often in the professional literature, yet they can be critical components of a child and young person's well-being, offering a source of strength and hope in trying circumstances.

Children for whom family and faith backgrounds are inseparable may need encouragement to feel comfortable in multi-faith settings. You need to address this dimension as part of the constellation of factors affecting black children and adolescents, bearing in mind the positive and sometimes negative impact spiritual or religious beliefs might have on their mental health. Children communicate about feelings and experiences more easily through responses to stories. Direct work that allows them to use their imaginations and access their own spirituality through stories can be liberating.

In a post-colonial world, the rights and expectations of indigenous people to reparation and how they are perceived are important issues in the context of achieving culturally competent practice. The disparities between developed and developing economies under the influence of globalisation are becoming more

Table 3.1: People born outside Great Britain and resident here, by countries of birth, 1991

Countries of birth	No. resident in Britain	% of Britain's population
Northern Ireland	245,000	0.45
Irish Republic	592,000	1.08
Germany	216,000	0.39
Italy	91,000	0.17
France	53,000	0.10
Other EC	133,900	0.24
Scandinavia and EFTA	58,300	0.11
E. Europe and former USSR	142,900	0.26
Cyprus	78,000	0.14
Rest of Near and Middle East	58,300	0.11
Aust, NZ and Canada	177,400	0.32
New Commonwealth	1,688,400	3.08
Jamaica	142,000	0.26
Rest of Caribbean	122,600	0.22
India	409,000	0.75
Pakistan	234,000	0.43
Bangladesh	105,000	0.19
Rest of South Asia	39,500	0.07
South East Asia	150,400	0.27
East Africa	220,600	0.40
West and Southern Africa	110,700	0.20
Rest of the World	566,200	1.03
Asia	231,000	0.42
North Africa	44,600	0.08
South Africa	68,000	0.12
Rest of Africa	34,300	0.06
USA	143,000	0.26
Rest of Americas	42,000	0.08
Total born outside GB	**3,991,000**	**7.27**

Owen, 1992-1995.

49

pronounced, incorporating new forms of cultural domination. The concept of cultural and social injustice can be illustrated thus (Powell, 2001):

- **Cultural domination** – some people are excluded because they are subjected to ways of interpreting or communicating which originate from a culture which is not their own, and which may be alien or hostile to them.

- **Non-recognition** – some people are excluded because they are effectively rendered invisible by the dominant cultural practices.

- **Cultural disrespect** – some people are excluded because they are routinely devalued by the stereotyping of public representations or everyday interactions within the dominant cultural context.

Activity 3.1

a) **Buy a selection of weekend newspapers and spend some time looking through them to see whether and how cultural diversity is represented.**

b) **Now consider the area or population your agency serves and ask yourself whether it is accessible to every member of the community.**

Understanding black and ethnic minority families

Institutionalised racism, failure of welfare services to listen to and respond to the concerns of black communities, stereotypical beliefs about black families, and barriers to access, all inhibit equal opportunity for black children with mental health problems to receive help. Practitioners attuned to anti-discriminatory values will be at an advantage over other professionals working in this area but you need to avoid complacency and collusion with covert institutional and personal racism. While it is important to avoid stereotypes of different black and ethnic minority families it is as important to understand that they each share in common the painful experiences as a consequence of endemic prejudice in a racist society.

The evidence demonstrating the prevention of initial and equal access and the inappropriateness of service provision has consistently been highlighted (Ely and Denney, 1987; Atkin and Rollings, 1993; DoH, 2000). However, there is not enough evidence that certain service characteristics are as relevant in their contribution to effectiveness in improving access as is frequently claimed. Cultural or ethnic congruence between service users and staff is perceived as a good strategy to improve service acceptability and accessibility. Yet there is no substantive body of evidence to support this, even though it instinctively feels right.

An evaluative approach such as that described by Courtney et al. (1996) suggests that differences in service provision outcomes should be assessed using robust evaluation designs. This is preferable rather than simply trying to recruit black staff en masse and assume service improvement will follow. Such an approach based on actual evidence can be employed to distinguish what works best for which black children and families, avoiding a colour-blind approach which evades the issue by claiming equal access to all regardless of race or cultural differences, or misguided attempts to provide culturally-sensitive but ineffective support.

Refugee and asylum seeking families experience additional stresses making them and their children highly vulnerable to mental health problems. They face relentless discrimination, racism, persecution, and suspicion from host countries that in many cases treat them as illegal immigrants, criminalising their attempts at survival. Studies of the psychological effects of homelessness on children are useful in measuring the potential impact on asylum seeking families housed in temporary accommodation (Heath, 1994; Amery, Tomkins and Victor, 1995; Vostanis, 1999). They demonstrate that these families constitute a high-risk group for the development of mental health problems and disorders. The stress caused by events precipitating their homelessness, combined with the trauma of displacement can undermine normal protective and resilience factors in both parents and children.

The disproportionate presence of black communities in areas of high social need means that specific economic and environmental factors should be identified when assessing families, and the mental health needs of their children, rather than relying on generalised ethnic differences (Shah, 1994). While working class families also receive inappropriate or ineffective services, the evidence that black children are less likely to access help, places them at a further disadvantage (Smaje, 1994; Dominelli, 1998). The characteristics of a service for black children and adolescents with mental health problems which aspires to better accessibility can be described as being composed of three elements:

- **Consultation** – with individual black families and their communities is required to ensure service provision meets their needs and to identify gaps in services. A pro-active community-oriented practice offers a practical and effective way of achieving this.

- **Information** – needs to be provided about rights and responsibilities in the context of childcare and mental health legislation. Jargon-free material should be accessible in different formats and languages about child and adolescent mental health needs.

- **Competence** – staff competence in child and adolescent mental health is not enough if this is not matched with demonstrable knowledge and skills required to practice in an ethnically diverse society.

The aim of culturally appropriate practice is to exclude the risk of misinterpretation or underplaying significant emotional and behavioural characteristics. In Britain the suicide rate among young men between the ages of 15 and 19 has more than doubled in the last 30 years. Worryingly, research has shown that in 60 per cent of these cases the young person had been demonstrating signs of emotional or behavioural difficulties for months before (McConville, 2001). The evidence demonstrates that black children are more likely to be perceived as physically aggressive in classrooms, and subsequently subject to racist stereotyping.

An understanding of the reluctance and resistance of parents to consider a mental health explanation for their child's behaviour or emotional state is particularly important when you are considering how to engage black and ethnic minority parents or carers in the process of support. Different cultural explanations based on physical or spiritual causation may need to be acknowledged, as well as fears of additional labelling marking out their children for further racist abuse. Denial, self-blame and guilt are powerful feelings generated at times of distress and bewilderment – a psycho-social perspective can help untangle these and enable parents or carers to move forward.

Activity 3.2

a) Together with a colleague find a copy of your agency's equal opportunities policy and discuss the implications for your own personal practice.

b) Each argues the case for and against a black member of staff being allocated to a black or other ethnic minority family.

The mental health needs of culturally diverse children

The evidence for the need to distinguish the different mental health needs of all children in a culturally diverse society and protect them from racist abuse is strong (Barter, 1999; Blackwell and Melzak, 2000; Chand, 2000; Weaver and Burns, 2001; Stanley, 2001). For example, refugee and asylum seeking children, some unaccompanied, many affected by extreme circumstances, might include those witnessing murder of parents or kin. They will also have experienced dislocation from school and community, severing of important friendships and extended family support, loss of home, and prolonged insecurity. These experiences will likely trigger symptoms consistent with post traumatic stress syndrome. This is manifested in a variety of ways including: shock, grief, depression, anxiety, hyperactivity, self-harming behaviour, anger, aggressive behaviour, fear, and guilt. Each individual child or adolescent will react differently according to variables such as:

- The context of their departure from the home country.

- The family cohesion and coping capacity.

- The child's own personality and predisposing psychological constitution.

- Proximity to extreme acts of murder or violence.

- The child's developmental stage and history of transition.

A number of studies compared levels of stress in adolescents and family functioning across different national boundaries including Canada, United States, Britain, Malaysia, India, Hong Kong and the Philippines (Bagley and Mallick, 1995; Bochner, 1994; Gibson-Cline, 1996; Watkins and Gerong, 1997; Martin, Rozanes, Pearce and Allison, 1995). A meta-analysis of these studies tested the hypothesis that while subjectively perceived levels of stress can vary significantly between cultures, the underlying causes of personal distress could be relatively similar between cultures (Bagley and Mallick, 2000). This is useful information for you to consider when trying to practice in culturally competent ways, that avoid racist stereotyping.

The differences in reported prevalence rates of mental health problems in various countries may reflect different classification systems, rather than real differences. Therefore, family dysfunction as perceived by the child or adolescent, with other perceived stressors, is a statistically significant predictor of various kinds of problem behaviours and emotional states in all ethnic groups. The conclusion is that there is a measurable, culturally universal, aspect of the relations of adolescents to family and other stress in terms of emotional and behavioural problems, and impaired self-esteem. However, a causal pattern from stress to mental health problems cannot be demonstrated beyond reasonable doubt.

The strongest evidence for prediction of mental health problems in children and adolescents across cultures, is that for general family stress (Bagley and Mallick, 2000). Looked at more closely this includes the effects of physical, sexual, and emotional abuse in the context of a climate of persistent negative family interactions. These findings are supported by other studies, which seek to illuminate and distinguish the particular factors influencing those children likely to develop mental health problems (Bagley and Young, 1998; Kashani and Allan, 1998; Vincent and Jouriles, 2000). When seeking to intervene effectively you have to carefully consider the various ways potential mental health problems are thought about, understood, and communicated in every family, in every culture.

It is argued that children do not have one essential identity, but switch identities in different situations and, subject to a diversity of cultural influences, can produce new identities (Ackroyd and Pilkington, 1999). By simply employing anti-racist and anti-discriminatory principles you may try to reinforce apparent cultural norms that are not applicable, or explain disturbed behaviour in terms of cultural features, which are irrelevant. This underlines the importance of understanding the culture within the culture – in other words finding out what are the individual and family norms, preferences, styles, habits and patterns of relationships that make that family what it is in the particular context of your involvement.

For example, there is an assumption that Asian families are close-knit with extended family relationships often living together in multi-generational households. This is a stereotype and may apply to a lot of Asian families but the danger is in applying the stereotype unthinkingly instead of using it to test a hypothesis about the particular family being helped. In many circumstances taking into account the concept of extended family relationships in close proximity can aid your assessment of emerging mental health problems in an Asian child or young person. But assuming this is always a sign of family strength and harmonious supportive relationships is risking missing obscure destructive dynamics that may be contributing to the child's mental health problems. These factors are beginning to emerge as some Asian youth struggle to balance loyalty to their history and culture with the different values and pressures in their environment (Qureshi et al., 2000; Fernando, 2002).

There is a fine balance between normalising behaviour attributed to various causal factors, and moving too quickly to apply or support a psychiatric diagnosis inappropriately. Each way of conceptualising the presenting problem has implications for the short and long-term outcomes of your assessment and intervention. A failure to recognise and acknowledge significant mental health problems could be just as damaging to the young person and others involved with them, as could seeking to explain their behaviour with a definitive psychiatric diagnosis. For some young people it could be a relief to have an explanation for feelings and behaviour that they find hard to make sense of, whereas for others it could exacerbate feelings of blame, guilt and self-loathing. The enduring social stigma of mental health problems in addition to racist experiences provides an overall context for these feelings to be repressed, displaced, or acted out.

Black and other ethnic minority children are disproportionately represented in the public care system. They have often been developmentally delayed, may have learning disabilities, have difficulty with communication, experience failure at school, and are at risk of beginning to establish persistent delinquent behaviours. Like many other children in the care system they face considerable hardship, which is built upon a history of failure, missed opportunity and psychological trauma. Their life opportunities and prospects are poor with a high risk of future psycho-social problems. Practitioners in residential care or in family placement teams need a perspective that fully embraces anti-racist practice combined with an appreciation of the mental health needs of this disadvantaged group of children.

Very little of the research on the mental health consequences of black and other ethnic minority children witnessing domestic violence has examined the impact race and racism might have on these children. It has been suggested that the societal context of racism provide these children with a sense of refuge inside their own home. However, when violence occurs inside their home as well, this can have profound effects on their sense of security and vulnerability, triggering acute anxiety-related symptoms (Imam, 1994). For these children there is no hiding place. Some of the negative impacts on black children are likely to be exacerbated by additional threats of abduction abroad, and/or by being asked inappropriately to act as interpreters or translators in situations where their welfare is at stake.

Activity 3.3

a) Write down a list of the ethnic minority groups in your community and against each one write a stereotypical characteristic relating to their personalities.

b) Now imagine two teenage girls, one white Irish, the other Pakistani, described as quiet, withdrawn and depressed. Think about the reasons for differences and similarities in your assessment and intervention plan.

Globalisation and emancipatory practice

The term globalisation has begun to feature in the professional literature reflecting profound shifts in the economic and social patterns of relationships between the richer industrialised countries and the poorer developing countries. It involves closer international economic integration prompted by the needs of Capitalism, but also has demographic, social, cultural and psychological dimensions (Midgley, 2001). Consistent with the link between the social context of child and adolescent mental health problems, it is therefore important that you consider the global context in terms of the challenges for building culturally competent practice.

Critics of globalisation argue that its impact is to maintain unequal power relationships between the richer and poorer countries so that patterns of wealth and consumer consumption in Europe and North America can be sustained. One of the side effects of this process is the standardisation and conformity required for consumer consumption patterns in order to maximise profit. The consequence is the steady and inexorable erosion of traditional markers of indigenous cultural identity combined with the elevation of global branding leaving black and ethnic minority children confused and vulnerable.

Dilemmas in trends towards cultural competence have been highlighted by reference to the practice of forced/arranged marriages and dowry, genital mutilation of children, and harsh physical punishments condoned by some societies (Midgley, 2001). These practices can be used to counter the argument for respecting ethnic and cultural diversity and support the notion of universal values as the basis for competent practice. Ethnic rivalries and the pride in national identity on which they are based also sit uneasily with culturally competent aspirations of international collaboration and mutual understanding.

However, rather than seek answers to these difficult issues in an introspective way, this emphasises the need for practitioners to reach out to the international welfare community with service users, to continue to debate, discuss and strive for ways to discover solutions. In the area of child and adolescent mental health, practitioners need to understand the impact such practices and the beliefs on which they are based are having on the mental health and emotional development of those adults promoting them and the children and young people experiencing them.

Cultural competence has been defined as developing skills in assessing the cultural climate of an organisation and being able to practice in a strategic manner within it. It has also been broadened to include *any* context in which staff practices in order to permit effective direct work at many levels (Baldwin, 2000; Fook, 2002). Whether at the strategic organisational level or the direct interpersonal level you can actively resist those pressures to conformity and routinised practice that in often discreet and inconspicuous ways, can undermine efforts to practise in culturally competent ways. The requirements of social justice demand vigilance and creativity in order to contribute towards an emancipatory practice that can liberate both staff and service users from prescribed practice orthodoxies. Such practice is the antithesis of stereotyped, one-dimensional thinking and is characterised by (Leonard, 1994):

- A commitment to standing alongside oppressed and impoverished populations.

- The importance of dialogic relations between workers and service users.

- Orientation towards the transformation of processes and structures that perpetuate domination and exploitation.

Components of a culturally competent practice

Cultural competence can be defined as a set of knowledge-based and interpersonal skills that allow individuals to understand, appreciate and work with individuals of cultures, from other than their own. Five components have been identified comprising culturally competent care (Kim, 1995):

- Awareness and acceptance of cultural differences.

- Capacity for cultural self-awareness.

- Understanding the dynamics of difference.

- Developing basic knowledge about the child's culture.

- Adapting practice skills to fit the cultural context of the child and family.

These are consistent with other work which critique the historical development of cross-cultural services and offer a model of service organisation and development designed to meet the needs of ethnic minority families (Moffic and Kinzie, 1996; Bhugra, 1999; Bhugra and Bahl, 1999). Ethnocentric and particularly Eurocentric, explanations of emotional and psychosocial development are not inclusive enough to understand the developments of diverse ethnic minority children. Failure to understand the cultural background of children and adolescents and their families can lead to unhelpful assessments, non-compliance, poor use of services, and alienation of the child and family from the welfare system (Dominelli, 1988).

Inspection of services for black children and their families shows that despite the rhetoric of anti-racist and anti-oppressive social work practice, assessments and care planning are generally inadequate (SSI, 2000). Assessments are often partial and rarely cover parental capacity, the child's needs, and environmental issues. There is little evidence that care planning takes a lifelong view – highlighting the failure to recruit black foster carers or understanding the changing characteristics of this group of children. The guidance suggests:

- Ensuring that services and staffing are monitored by ethnicity to ensure they are provided appropriately and equally.

- Involving ethnic minorities in planning and reviewing services.

- Training in anti-racist and anti-discriminatory practice.

- Investigating and monitoring complaints of racial discrimination or harassment.

- Explicit policies are in place for working with black families.

Your interpersonal skills in facilitating service user empowerment particularly with children and adolescent mental health problems are indicated in any vision of the future shape of service provision (Walker, 2001). Community work and group work are also required to enable families and young people to support each other and raise collective awareness of shared issues. Investigation of indigenous healing practices and beliefs provide a rich source of information to utilise in the helping process. Advocacy skills, in which young people are encouraged to be supported and represented by advocates of their choice, would help contribute to influencing current service provision (Ramon, 1999).

The notion that practitioners should respect diversity, build on an ethnic group's strengths and provide for individual and social change, is not new (Pentini and Lorenz, 1996). Yet there is a considerable gap in the literature on effectiveness in general, and specifically, working with black and ethnic minority clients. Reviews of practice highlight the need for more rigorous evaluation of what works with which clients in what circumstances with what methods (Russell, 1990; Thompson, 1995; Shaw, 1996; Cheetham, 1997). Translating research findings into practice in the context of child and adolescent mental health services can contribute to a more holistic response to the needs of every child and family that requires it. This can help towards offering black citizens an equal opportunity to take their rightful place in society and benefit from its resources.

Culturally competent practice demands that above all you do not avoid the challenge of developing a perspective on child development that recognises the plurality of pathways to maturity within that perspective. In other words it is not good enough to rely on a limited, partial understanding of child development to be applied universally as a measure against which to judge a child's emotional and psychological progress. The influence of North American and Eurocentric child psychology literature and theories is extending beyond those societies from which dominant discourses have been generated. Child development experts have tailored professional guidance in developing countries to explicitly assimilate western child development theory into Third World contexts. Industrialising countries with formerly agricultural histories have a rich reservoir of cultural and familial practices to draw from to inform their understanding of their children's emotional and behavioural development.

Many traditional beliefs and practices are under pressure nowadays under the inexorable momentum of economic and cultural globalisation forcing parents to change attitudes, values, habits and child rearing practices. The consequences for family stability and child and adolescent mental health are traumatic (James and Prout, 1997). Use of the Assessment framework described in the last chapter requires that child and family differences must be approached with knowledge and sensitivity in a non-judgemental way. The danger is that fear, ignorance, and institutional and personal racism can result in a lack of accuracy and balance in analysing a child or young person's needs. You need to:

- Employ multiple cultural assumptions to understand the child and family circumstances.

- Increase your sensitivity to racial and cultural variations within groups and between individuals.

- Always base your assumptions on evidence.

- Take account of the barriers that prevent the social integration of black families.

- Compare your interpretation of symptoms with the child and family members.

Wherever you work, and in whatever practice orientation, your task is to maintain a critical but constructive perspective on your agency's treatment of black and ethnic minority children and young people. Voluntary projects and family support services organised by charities and church groups attempt to meet sometimes-complex needs, on few resources and continual uncertainty over future funding. Assessment and interpretation of behaviour through the spectrum of child developmental milestones that are culturally adapted are required to improve the recognition of potential mental health problems in black children and refer on to specialist resources if necessary. The full range of intellectual and therapeutic resources available is needed to begin the process of assessment and intervention in harmony with appropriate multi-agency co-operation and participation. Often in these circumstances the resource that can make a big difference to whether an emerging problem becomes a larger and entrenched problem is the availability of consultation or supervision.

Activity 3.4

a) **Pick three specific elements of culturally competent practice that are the most important to you.**

b) **Now make an action plan to put into practice those three elements and review your progress in three months time.**

■ LEARNING REVIEW

In this chapter we have examined the concept of culturally competent practice in relation to the needs of black and ethnic minority children and adolescents who have mental health problems in addition to experiencing personal and institutional racism in Britain.

We have considered the disproportionate representation of black children in the public care system and examined some of the evidence that demonstrates the inequitable and discriminatory services offered to black and other ethnic minority children and families.

We have reflected on the way stereotyping of different cultures can affect our assessment of the mental health needs of culturally diverse children. The risks in ascribing mental health problems to indigenous beliefs or vice versa have been highlighted. Western concepts of illness have been contrasted with non-western beliefs, customs and practices that need to be borne in mind when working with black and other ethnic minority children and young people.

We have illuminated the connection between culturally competent practice and the wider context of globalisation and emancipatory practice. This can explain the pressures on different cultural groups to conform to practices that create tension and stress within families. The components of a culturally competent practice have been elucidated to provide a resource to help achieve a balanced and appropriate response to the mental health needs of a culturally diverse society.

References and further reading

Ackroyd J and Pilkington A (1999) Childhood and the Construction of Ethnic Identities in a Global Age. *Childhood.* 6: 4, 443-54.

Amery J, Tomkins A and Victor C (1995) The Prevalence of Behavioural Problems Amongst Homeless Primary School Children in an Outer London Borough: A Feasibility Survey. *Public Health.* 109: 421-4.

Atkin K and Rollings J (1993) *Community Care in a Multi-Racial Britain: A Critical Review of the Literature.* London, HMSO.

Bagley C and Mallick K (1995) Negative Self Perception and Components of Stress in Canadian, British and Hong Kong Adolescents. *Perceptual Motor Skills.* 81: 123-7.

Bagley C and Mallick K (2000) How Adolescents Perceive Their Emotional Life, Behaviour, and Self-Esteem in Relation to Family Stressors: A Six-Culture Study. In Singh N, Leung J and Singh A. *International Perspectives on Child and Adolescent Mental Health.* Oxford, Elsevier.

Bagley C and Young L (1998) The Interactive Effects of Physical, Emotional, and Sexual Abuse on Adjustment in a Longtitudinal Cohort of 565 Children From Birth to Age 17. In Bagley C and Mallick K (Eds.) *Child Sexual Abuse: New Theory and Research.* Aldershot, Ashgate.

Baldwin M (2000) *Care Management and Community Care.* Aldershot, Ashgate.

Barter C (1999) *Protecting Children From Racism and Racist Abuse: A Research Review.* London, NSPCC.

Bhugra D (1999) *Mental Health of Ethnic Minorities.* London, Gaskell.

Bhugra D and Bahl V (1999) *Ethnicity: An Agenda for Mental Health.* London, Gaskell.

Bhui K (1997) London's Ethnic Minorities and The Provision of Mental Health Services. In Johnson et al. (Eds.) *London's Mental Health.* London, King's Fund Institute.

Bhui K and Olajide D (1999) *Mental Health Service Provision for a Multi-Cultural Society.* London, Saunders.

Blackwell D and Melzak S (2000) *Far From the Battle But Still at War-Troubled Refugee Children in School.* London, The Child Psychotherapy Trust.

Bochner S (1994) Cross-Cultural Differences in The Self-Concept: A Test of Hofstede's Individualism/Collectivism Distinction. *Journal of Cross-Cultural Psychology.* 2: 273-83.

Chand A (2000) The Over Representation of Black Children in The Child Protection System: Possible Causes,Consequences and Solutions. *Child and Family Social Work.* 5: 67-77.

Cheetham J (1997) The Research Perspective. In Davies M (Ed.) *The Blackwell Companion to Social Work.* Oxford, Blackwell.

Cole E, Leavey G and King M (1995) Pathways to Care for Patients With First Episode of Psychosis. A Comparison of Ethnic Groups. *British Journal of Psychiatry.* 167: 770-6.

Courtney M et al. (1996) Race and Child Welfare Services: Past Research and Future Directions. *Child Welfare.* LXXV: 2, Mar/Apr.

Cross T et al. (1989) *Toward a Culturally Competent System of Care: A Monograph on Effective Services for Minority Children Who Are Severely Emotionally Disturbed.* Washington DC, Georgetown University Child Development Center.

DoH (2000) *Social Services Inspectorate: Excellence Not Excuses: Inspection of Services for Ethnic Minority Children and Families.* London, HMSO.

Dominelli L (1988) *Anti-Racist Social Work.* Basingstoke, Macmillan.

Dominelli L (1998) Anti-Oppressive Practice in Context. In Adams R, Dominelli L and Payne M (Eds.) *Social Work: Themes, Issues and Critical Debates.* Basingstoke, Macmillan.

Ely P and Denney P (1987) *Social Work in a Multi-Racial Society.* London, Gower.

Fernando S (2002) *Mental Health Race and Culture.* Basingstoke, Palgrave.

Fook J (2002) *Social Work: Critical Theory and Practice.* London, Sage.

Gibson-Cline J (Ed.) (1996) *Adolescence: From Crisis to Coping.* London, Butterworth-Heinemann.

Heath I (1994) The Poor Man at His Gate: Homelessness Is an Avoidable Cause of Ill Health. *British Medical Journal.* 309: 1675-6.

Imam U (1994) Asian Children and Domestic Violence. In Mullender A and Morley R (Eds.) *Children Living With Domestic Violence.* London, Whiting and Birch.

James A and Prout A (Eds.) (1990) *Constructing and Reconstructing Childhood.* Basingstoke, Falmer.

Kashani J and Allan W (1998) *The Impact of Family Violence on Children and Adolescents*. London, Sage.

Kim W J (1995) A Training Guideline of Cultural Competence for Child and Adolescent Psychiatric Residencies. *Child Psychiatry and Human Development*. 26: 2, 125-36.

Leonard P (1997) *Postmodern Welfare: Reconstructing an Emancipatory Project*. London, Sage.

Martin G et al. (1995) Adolescent Suicide, Depression and Family Dysfunction. *Acta Psychiatrica Scandinavica*. 92: 336-44.

McConville B (2001) *Saving Young Lives: Calls to Childline About Suicide*. London, Childline.

Midgley J (2001) Issues in International Social Work-Resolving Critical Debates in the Profession. *Journal of Social Work*. 1: 1, 21-35.

Moffic H and Kinzie J (1996) The History and Future of Cross-Cultural Psychiatric Services. *Community Mental Health Journal*. 32: 6, 581-92.

Pentini-Aluffi A and Lorenz W (1996) *Anti Racist Work With Young People*. Lyme Regis, Russell House.

Powell F (2001) *The Politics of Social Work*. London, Sage.

Qureshi T, Berridge D and Wenman H (2000) *Where to Turn? Family Support for South Asian Communities: A Case Study*. London, National Children's Bureau/JRF.

Ramon S (1999) Social Work. In Bhui K and Olajide D (Eds.) *Mental Health Service Provision for a Multi-cultural Society*. London. Saunders.

Russell M (1990) *Clinical Social Work: Research and Practice*. Newbury Park, Sage.

Shah R (1994) Practice With Attitude: Questions on Cultural Awareness Training. *Child Health*, April/May.

Shaw I (1996) *Evaluating in Practice*. Aldershot, Arena.

Smaje C (1995) *Health, Race and Ethnicity: Making Sense of the Evidence*. London, Kings Fund Institute.

Stanley K (2001) *Cold Comfort: Young Separated Refugees in England*. London, Save The Children.

Thompson N (1995) *Theory and Practice in Health and Social Welfare*. Buckingham, Open University Press.

Vincent J and Jouriles E (Eds.) (2000) *Domestic Violence: Guidelines for Research Informed Practice*. London, Jessica Kingsley.

Vostanis P and Cumella S (1999) *Homeless Children: Problems and Needs.* London, Jessica Kingsley.

Walker S (2001) Consulting With Children and Young People. *The International Journal of Children's Rights.* 9: 45-56.

Watkins D and Gerong A (1997) Culture and Spontaneous Self-Concepts Among Filipino College Students. *Journal of Social Psychology.* 137: 480-8.

Weaver H and Burns B (2001) I Shout With Fear at Night – Understanding The Traumatic Experiences of Refugee and Asylum Seekers. *Journal of Social Work.* 1: 2, 147-64.

Chapter 4
The organisational and legal context

Learning objectives

- Describe the four tier model of CAMHS organisation.

- Describe the main legislative framework for CAMHS.

- Explain how CAMHS fits with other children's services.

- Identify how different agencies conceptualise children and young people's mental health problems.

Introduction

In 1997 the House of Commons Health Committee Fourth Report on Expenditure, Administration, and Policy, focused on child and adolescent mental health services. This took place in the context of demands from parents, and staff in education, health and social work services overwhelmed by needs they were unable to meet (House of Commons, 1997). The committee noted the significance of mental health as one of five key areas in the Conservative Government's Health of the Nation programme. It suggested that the Department of Health should adopt indicators and targets for children, including the setting of a target to reduce child suicides, and a target for the reduction of specific disorders.

Later in 1997 the new Labour government pledged itself to change the NHS internal market and lay the foundation for a new approach based on co-operation rather than competition between all stakeholders. The aim was to promote partnership as one of the key strategic commissioning objectives to deliver best outcomes for local populations from the resources available to them (DoH, 1997). Assembling the findings of three influential pieces of research and combining them with government policy statements, enabled the design of a set of guidelines for CAMH service providers as shown in Table 4.1 (Kurtz, 1992; Kurtz et al., 1994; HAS, 1995; Audit Commission, 1998).

Table 4.1: CAMHS service provider guidelines

Relationships with commissioners

- The service should be represented on a group that regularly advises commissioners and purchasers about arrangements for delivering comprehensive child and adolescent mental health services.
- The CAMHS should have a plan which reflects an understanding of how the purchaser perceives the contribution of this specialist service as part of the delivery of the full child and adolescent mental health service.

Top level trust planning

- There should be an operational policy for CAMHS.
- There should be a recognisable and separate budget for the CAMHS.
- There should be an awareness of the major elements of CAMHS expenditure.
- Services should be child-centred and responsive to age-related and other particular needs, such as those of families from minority ethnic groups.
- Services should have protocols for dealing with confidentiality.
- Services should be provided in a welcoming environment, with buildings and rooms safe and suitable for children and young people.
- There should be service level agreements to cover consultancy and advice for consultant colleagues in other specialties such as paediatrics. Agreements should ensure that the service provides regular and adequate input to children's homes, EBD schools, secure units, and to other groups of young people at particular risk.
- There should be provision for adequate specialist mental health support to social workers, teachers, GPs and others.
- The CAMHS should be provided by a multi-disciplinary team or through a network. Health service personnel will make up only a part of the team – appropriate input from social services and education departments should also be maintained.
- There should be a clear relationship with adult mental health services.

Operations

- There should be an adequate information system geared specifically to CAMHS.
- The service should offer a relevant range of interventions to suit different needs.
- There should be clear referral channels to CAMHS which are appropriate to the referrer.
- There should be a clear access route to day patient and in-patient services.
- There should be a clear protocol for dealing with young people who present in crisis – including those who may deliberately harm themselves. There should be access to adequate and appropriately skilled 24 hour cover by mental health specialists for the child and adolescent population.
- Waiting time for the first appointment for a non-urgent condition should be less than 13 weeks.
- The service should identify topics for audit which should be undertaken regularly.
- Appropriate training should be offered to CAMHS staff, including secretarial and reception staff.

Audit Commission, 1998.

The need for such guidelines had been an important step towards establishing some commonality and equity in service provision. Mental health services for children and adolescents are generally poorly planned and historically determined rather than needs led. Their geographical distribution is patchy and they are variable in quality and composition. The work they do often seems unrelated in strength or diversity to assessed population need. Child and adolescent mental health services comprise the specifically trained resources in child and adolescent mental health available for a particular population. In 1995 CAMHS were found to be managed and delivered often in more than one health trust, and in more than one agency, thwarting attempts to co-ordinate care (HAS, 1995). Services for the mental health of children and adolescents aim to:

- Promote mental health in young people.

- Prevent problems occurring.

- Treat and manage problems and disorders that do arise so that their adverse impacts are minimised.

Organisational context

The national picture in child and adolescent mental health services is still characterised by long waiting times, and uneven distribution of specialist provision. Obscure access routes for service user pathways combine with excessive pressure on primary preventive services in health and social care, resulting in poor levels of inter-agency co-operation. The outcome is to create barriers to those most disadvantaged and socially excluded families requiring help. The government's *National Priorities Guidance, Modernising Health and Social Services* (1998) states that one of its mental health objectives is to:

> *Improve provision of appropriate high quality care and treatment for children and young people by building up locally-based child and adolescent mental health services. This should be achieved through ... improved liaison between primary care, specialist CAMHS, social services and other agencies.*

This was the first time that National Priorities Guidance was directed jointly at local authorities and health authorities. Local authorities were given the lead on children's welfare and interagency working. Local authorities and health authorities were to share lead on mental health and reducing health inequalities. There is evidence of similar developments aimed at preventing mental health difficulties progressing, and responding quickly to those that occur (Nixon and Northrup, 1997).

The National Service Framework for Mental Health was introduced in 2000 to try to address inequities and bring cohesion to services for mentally ill people. However the NSF did not include children and adolescents within its remit. At the time of writing the current plan is to bring child and adolescent mental health services into the National Service Framework for Children due to be published in 2003. The national children's mental health charity 'Young Minds' has warned that excluding CAMHS from the NSF for Mental Health was a missed opportunity (Young Minds, 2001). Including it within what will necessarily be a broad NSF for Children, will dilute or obscure the current work being undertaken to improve services for this traditionally neglected area of children's lives.

For the time being the current organisational structure of child and adolescent mental health services can be represented by Table 4.2 which illustrates the four tier progressive framework through which children and young people will be referred. Practitioners, whether in statutory or voluntary organisations may be involved at any of the four Tiers of intervention, but the majority will be involved at Tier 1 and Tier 2. Most children or adolescents with mental health problems will be seen at Tiers 1 and 2. All agencies should have structures in place to facilitate the referral of clients between tiers, and to maximise the contribution of CAMH specialists at each tier. The importance of multi-professional and inter-agency working cannot be over-emphasised in this area of work.

Activity 4.1

a) Examine Table 4.2 and find out where your agency is placed in the CAMHS structure.

b) Find out from your line manager or agency guidelines what the protocols are for referring children and adolescents between the four-tier CAMHS structure.

Legal framework

The legal framework for child and adolescent mental health encompasses a wide spectrum of social policy including juvenile justice, mental health, education, and children and family legislation. The term 'mental illness' is not defined in law relating to children and young people. The variety of legal frameworks affecting

Table 4.2: CAMHS tiered framework

Key components, professionals and functions of tiered child and adolescent mental health services	
Tier 1. A primary level which includes interventions by: • GPs • health visitors • school nurses • social services • voluntary agencies • teachers • residential social workers • juvenile justice workers Child and adolescent mental health services (CAMHS) at this level are provided by non-specialists who are in a position to: • Identify mental health problems early in their development. • Offer general advice – and in certain cases treatment for less severe problems. • Pursue opportunities for promoting mental health and preventing mental health problems.	**Tier 3. A specialist service for the more severe, complex and persistent disorders. This is usually a multi-disciplinary team or service working in a community child mental health clinic or child psychiatry out-patient service, and including:** • child and adolescent psychiatrists • social workers • clinical psychologists • community psychiatric nurses • child psychotherapists • occupational therapists • art, music and drama therapists The core CAMHS in each district should be able to offer: • Assessment and treatment of child mental health disorders. • Assessment for referrals to Tier 4. • Contribution to the services, consultation and training at Tiers 1 and 2. • Participation in R and D projects.
Tier 2. A level of service provided by uni-professional group which relates to others through a network (rather than within a team). These include: • clinical child psychologists • paediatricians, especially community • educational psychologists • child psychiatrists • community child psychiatric nurses • nurse specialists CAMHS professionals should be able to offer: • Training and consultation to other professionals (who might be within Tier 1). • Consultation for professionals and families. • Outreach to identify severe or complex needs which require more specialist interventions but where the children or families are unwilling to use specialist services. • Assessment which may trigger treatment at a different tier.	**Tier 4. Access to infrequently used but essential tertiary level services such as day units, highly specialist out-patient teams, and in-patient units for older children and adolescents who are severely mentally ill or at suicidal risk. These services may need to be provided on a supra-district level as not all districts can expect to offer this level of expertise.** The most specialist CAMHS may provide for more than one district or region, and should be able to offer a range of services which might include: • adolescent in-patient units • secure forensic adolescent units • eating disorder units • specialist teams for sexual abuse • specialist teams for neuro-psychiatric problems

Based on *A Handbook on Child and Adolescent Mental Health*, DoH and DoE, 1995.

them provide the context for work undertaken by a number of health and social care staff concerned about children and young people whose behaviour is described as disturbed or disturbing. The relevant legal and ethical issues for practitioners are linked to practice principles and values embedded in a psycho-social approach. Of particular interest to practitioners in the context of empowering practice are the issues of consent and confidentiality. The Children's Legal Centre (1994) draws attention to a number of issues regarding the rights of children and young people who might have contact with agencies on the basis of their mental health problems:

- Lack of knowledge and implementation of legal rights for children and young people to control their own medical treatment, and a general lack of rights to self-determination.

- Discrimination against children and young people on grounds of disability, race, culture, colour, language, religion, gender, and sexuality which can lead to categorisation as mentally ill and subsequent intervention and detention.

- Unnecessary and in some cases unlawful restriction of liberty and inadequate safeguards in mental health and other legislation for children and young people.

- Inadequate assessment and corresponding lack of care, treatment and education in the criminal justice system.

- Use of drugs for containment rather than treatment purposes in the community, schools, and in other institutions, combined with a lack of knowledge of consent procedures.

- Placement of children on adult wards in psychiatric hospitals.

- Lack of clear ethical guidelines for extreme situations such as force-feedings in cases of anorexia, care of suicide risk young people, and care of HIV positive or AIDS patients.

Mental Health Act 1983

The Mental Health Act 1983, the Children Act 1989 and the Human Rights Act 1998, are currently the three significant pieces of legislation providing the context for practice in child and adolescent mental health. The Mental Health Act 1983 is a piece of legislation designed mainly for adults with mental health problems and amongst other things set the framework for the assessment and potential compulsory admission of patients to hospital. The majority of children in psychiatric hospitals or units are informal patients. They do not have the same access to safeguards available to adult patients detained under the Mental Health

Act 1983. Children under 16 are frequently admitted by their parents even though they may not have wanted to be admitted. This is de facto detention. The number of children admitted to NHS psychiatric units has risen in recent years. In 1995, 4,891 children and young people under 19 were admitted in England. By 2000 the number had risen to 5,788, an increase of 18 per cent.

Parts of the Mental Health Act 1983 provide for compulsory admission and continued detention where a child or young person is deemed to have, or suspected of having, a mental disorder. The mental disorder must be specified as mental illness, psychopathic disorder, learning disability, or severe mental impairment. Learning disability is not stated as such in the Act, and as with psychopathic disorder, it must be associated with abnormally aggressive or seriously irresponsible conduct. Full assessment and treatment orders under Sections 2 and 3 require an application to be made by the nearest relative or a social worker approved under the Mental Health Act, together with medical recommendation by two doctors. The sections of the Mental Health Act 1983 most likely to be used with children and young people are:

- Section 2   for assessment for possible admission for up to 28 days.

- Section 4   for an emergency assessment for up to 72 hours admission.

- Section 5 (2)   for emergency detention by one doctor for up to 72 hours.

- Section 5 (4)   for emergency six hour detention when no doctor or social worker available.

- Section 3   for inpatient treatment for a treatable disorder for up to six months.

Children Act 1989

A child who is suffering with mental health problems may behave in ways that stretch their parents' or carer's capacity to cope which can result in the potential for significant harm. On the other hand a child who is being abused or neglected may come to the attention of professionals concerned initially about their mental health. The interactive nature of mental health and child abuse presents a considerable challenge for practitioners tasked with conducting assessment work in child and family contexts. This issue is explored in more depth in Chapter 2. The duties under the terms of the Children Act are straightforward and underpinned by the following principles:

- The welfare of the child is paramount.

- Children should be brought up and cared for within their own families wherever possible.

- Children should be safe and protected by effective interventions if at risk.

- Courts should avoid delay and only make an order if this is better than not making an order.

- Children should be kept informed about what happens to them and involved in decisions made about them.

- Parents continue to have parental responsibility for their children even when their children are no longer living with them.

Together with the four-tier integrated child and adolescent mental health services structure, the framework is there to achieve better co-ordination and effectiveness of services to help any family with a child who has a mental health problem. This is made clear under the terms of Section 17 of the Children Act that lays a duty on local authorities to provide services for children in need. The definition of 'in need' has three elements:

1. The child is unlikely to achieve or maintain, or to have the opportunity of achieving or maintaining, a reasonable standard of health or development without the provision for the child of services by a local authority.

2. The child's health or development is likely to be significantly impaired, or further impaired, without provision for the child of such services.

3. The child is disabled.

The Act further defines disability to include children suffering from mental disorder of any kind. In relation to the first two parts of the definition, health or development is defined to cover physical, intellectual, emotional, social or behavioural development and physical or mental health. These concepts are open to interpretation of what is meant by a 'reasonable standard of health and development', as well as the predictive implications for children having the 'opportunity' of achieving or maintaining it. However it is reasonable to include the following groups of children within this part of the definition of in need and to argue the case for preventive support where there is a risk of children developing mental health problems (Ryan, 1999):

- children living in poverty

- homeless children

- children suffering the effects of racism

- young carers

- delinquent children

- children separated from parents

- young people isolated in rural areas

Section 47 of The Children Act gives the local authority a duty to investigate where they suspect a child is suffering or is likely to suffer significant harm. Guidance suggests the purpose of such an investigation is to establish facts, decide if there are grounds for concern, identify risk, and decide protective action. The problem with child and adolescent mental health problems is that this guidance assumes certainty within a time-limited assessment period. The nature of emotional and behavioural difficulties is their often hidden quality combined with the child's own reluctance to acknowledge them. The interpretation of a child or young person's emotional or behavioural state is usually decided by a child and adolescent psychiatrist who may be brought into a Section 43 child assessment order that has been sought following parental lack of co-operation. The social worker in situations like this, and in full care proceedings, has a crucial role in balancing the need to protect the child with the future consequences on them and their family of oppressive investigations and interventions.

Human Rights Act 1998

The Human Rights Act (UN, 1998) came into force in 2000 and incorporates into English law most of the provisions of the European Convention on Human Rights. The Act applies to all authorities undertaking functions of a public nature, including all care providers in the public sector. The Human Rights Act supports the protection and improvement of the health and welfare of children and young people throughout the United Kingdom.

Article 3 concerns freedom from torture and inhuman or degrading treatment. Children and young people who have been subjected to restraint, seclusion, or detention as a result of alarming behaviour could use this part of the Act to raise complaints.

Article 5 concerns the right to liberty, and together with Article 6 concerning the right to a fair hearing, are important to children and young people detained under a section of the Mental Health Act, the Children Act, or within the youth justice system. Practitioners involved in such work must ensure that detention is based on sound opinion, in accordance with clearly laid out legal procedure accessible to the individual, and only lasts for as long as the mental health problem persists.

Article 8 guarantees the right to privacy and family life. Refugees and asylum seeking families can become entangled in complex legal procedures relating to citizenship and entitlement. Practitioners attuned to the attachment relationships of often small children can use this knowledge to support Article 8 proceedings. In such circumstances the maintenance of the family unit is paramount.

Article 10 concerns basic rights to freedom of expression and in the context of children's mental health, is a crucial safeguard to ensuring that practitioners work actively to enable children and young people to express their opinions about service provision.

Article 14 states that all children have an equal claim to the rights set out in the Convention 'irrespective of the child's or his or her parent's or legal guardian's race, colour, sex, language, religion, political or other opinion, national, ethnic or social origin, property, disability, birth or other status'. This provision could be used to argue for equality of service provision and non-prejudicial diagnosis or treatment. You need to ensure you are employing anti-racist and non-discriminatory practice as well as facilitating children and young people to:

- Access information about their rights.

- Contact mental health services.

- Access advocates and children's rights organisations.

- Create children's service user groups.

To do this you need to get to know your patch, community, neighbourhood or locality and find out what young people are doing, what their interests are, and what bothers them. It is as important to make contact with those who are extrovert as those who are withdrawing and becoming distant from peer contact. You need to think beyond your organisational constraints and make links with others concerned enough to want to do something positive to help, rather than seek to blame and punish the consequences of some young people's unacceptable behaviour.

Activity 4.2

a) Together with a colleague review the above material relating to the legal context of CAMHS. Each of you draws up a list of the three most important points. Discuss and compare your answers.

b) Think about a child or young person you have recently helped and draw a diagram showing the number of agencies involved with them and their legal context.

Consent and confidentiality

Defining the capacity of a child to make her or his own decisions and consent to intervention is not easy especially in the area of child and adolescent mental health. The concept of 'Gillick competent' arose following a landmark ruling in 1985 in the House of Lords (3 All E.R. 402, 1985). That ruling held that competent children under 16 years of age can consent to and refuse advice and treatment from a doctor. Since then further court cases have modified the Gillick principle so that if either the child or any person with parental responsibility gives consent to treatment, doctors can proceed, even if one or more of these people, including the child, disagree.

The concept of competent refers to a child having the capacity to understand the nature, terms and consequences of proposed treatment, or the consequences of refusing such treatment, free from pressure to comply. In practice, children are considered to be lacking in capacity to consent although this could be as a result of underestimating children's intelligence, or more likely, reflect an inability to communicate effectively with them. Courts have consistently held that children do not have sufficient understanding of death – hence the force-feeding of anorexics and blood transfusions of Jehovah's Witnesses.

Court of Appeal decisions have since overturned the principle that Gillick competent children can refuse treatment. Such cases involved extreme and life-threatening situations involving anorexia, blood transfusion, and severely disturbed behaviour. Importantly, the courts have indicated that any person with parental responsibility can in certain circumstances override the refusal of a Gillick competent child. This means that children under a care order or accommodated by the local authority even if considered not to have the capacity to consent, still retain the right to be consulted about proposed treatment. If a child is accommodated the social worker should always obtain the parents' consent since they retain full parental responsibility (Brammer, 2003). If the child is under a care order the parents share parental responsibility with the local authority. Good practice requires the practitioner in these situations to negotiate with parents about who should give consent and ensure that all views are recorded in the care plan.

Children and young people require the help and advice of a wide variety of sources at times of stress and unhappiness in their lives. There are voluntary, statutory and private agencies as well as relatives or friends who they find easier to approach than parents. They may want to talk in confidence about worrying feelings or behaviour. The legal position in these circumstances is confused, with agencies and professional groups relying on voluntary codes of practice guidance. A difficult dilemma frequently arises when children are considering whether a helping service is acceptable while the staff are required to disclose information to others in certain situations, for example where child protection concerns are aroused.

The agency policies should be accessible to children and clearly state the limits to confidentiality. But in doing so many practitioners know they could be discouraging the sharing of important feelings and information. The importance of establishing trust and confidence in vulnerable young people and constantly having to tread the line between facilitating sensitive communication and selecting what needs to be passed on to parents, colleagues or to third parties is not easy. Ideally, where disclosure needs to be made against a young person's wishes it is good practice to inform the young person in advance and give her or him the chance to disclose the information first.

The Data Protection Act 1984 and The Access to Personal Files Act 1987 give individuals the right to see information about them, with some limitations. Children 'of sufficient understanding' have the right of access except in certain circumstances. These are particularly relevant to child and adolescent mental health where:

- Disclosure would be likely to cause serious harm to the child's physical or mental health.
- The information would disclose the identity of another person.
- The information is contained within a court report.
- The information is restricted or prohibited from disclosure in adoption cases.
- The information is a statement of special education needs made under the Education Act 1981.

Activity 4.3

a) **Think about a time in your childhood when you felt worried or very upset about something but were unable to talk to anyone about it. Looking back, what would you liked to have happened or what would you have liked a trusted adult to say to you which would have enabled you to talk?**

b) **Find a copy of your employer's policy on client confidentiality or talk to your line manager about the issue and any guidelines that are available. Discuss who to contact when dilemmas about confidentiality occur.**

Inter-agency conceptual thinking

Historically, there have been difficulties in collaboration in the area of child and adolescent mental health which undermine the strategic aim of fostering closer working. These difficulties can be explained in terms of resource constraints combined with extra demands continually being placed on all statutory agencies. Other explanations emphasise in addition:

- The different theoretical models and values underpinning working practices.

- The importance of personality factors.

- The historical and haphazard development of responses.

- The capacity of senior managers to create an atmosphere of co-operation at all levels of the system (Pearce, 1999).

Children with mental health problems may move between four overlapping systems: criminal justice, social services, education and the health service. Children are not always helped by the appropriate service since this often depends on the resources available in the area at the time. It also depends on how different professional staff may perceive the behaviour of a particular child, and the vocabulary used by the service in which they work.

A youth offending team member may talk about a young person engaged in anti-social activity, a teacher about poor concentration and aggressive behaviour, and a social worker or youth worker may perceive a needy, anxious, abused child. All are describing the same child.

The pathway of a child into these systems is crucial because the consequences for subsequent intervention can either exacerbate the behaviour or help to reduce it. Table 4.3 illustrates schematically potential agency responses to the same presenting problem. The Crime and Disorder Act 1998 and the Special Educational Needs and Disability Act 2001 provide the legislative framework for youth justice and children with special educational needs. In both cases, children and young people with mental health problems may find they are being inappropriately dealt with under these Acts. The long-term consequences for acquiring a pejorative label such as trouble-maker, delinquent or aggressive can be negative.

Some children from these groups may be truanting from school, getting involved in criminal activities, or have behaviour problems at school or at home. Agency responses will tend to address the presenting problem and present an intervention to address it. Assessment of the needs of individual children and families is often

77

Table 4.3: Agency responses to the same presenting problem

Juvenile justice	Social services	Education	Psychiatry
Aggression	Aggression	Aggression	Aggression
Referral to police: decision to charge ↓	Referral to social services ↓	Referral to education department ↓	Referral to child psychiatrist ↓
Pre-sentence report completed ↓	Social work assessment conducted ↓	Educational psychology assessment ↓	Psychiatric assessment ↓
Sentenced to custody ↓	Decision to accommodate ↓	Placed in residential school ↓	Admitted to regional in-patient unit ↓
Labelled as young offender	Labelled as beyond parental control	Labelled as having learning difficulty	Labelled as mentally ill

After Malek, 1993.

cursory, deficit-oriented, punitive and static. The pressure to complete fast assessments in short time scales inhibits the creation of a thoughtful, helping relationship with a young person. Important information can be overlooked or missed altogether that would better inform the way forward. Using interpersonal skills and providing the right conditions, including time and patience, a skilled practitioner can help a child or adolescent open up. The new *Framework for the Assessment of Children in Need* (2001) offers the opportunity for practitioners to conduct more positive, comprehensive assessments that permit the mental health needs of children and adolescents to be illuminated.

Activity 4.4

a) Select a child or young person you have worked with and write down the main reasons for the referral to your agency and the initial assessment. Now imagine you worked in two different agencies with the same client and write down the assessment from their two different agency perspectives.

b) Now write one referral and one assessment using the language of the child or young person as they would describe their problems.

■ LEARNING REVIEW

In this chapter we have examined the organisational structure and legal context of child and adolescent mental health services. The four-tier structure is the preferred model currently in operation where children's mental health problems are managed progressively from the primary Tier 1 through to the specialist Tier 4 level.

The legal context of child and adolescent mental health services embraces The 1983 Mental Health Act, The 1989 Children Act and the 1998 Human Rights Act. Within these statutes the mental health status of children and young people is described in relation to compulsory action. Children's legal rights in relation to their needs and protection are exemplified. The legislation also describes the situation with regard to consent, confidentiality and complaints.

We have considered how important inter-agency co-operation is in effective CAMHS, and how different agencies can perceive and conceptualise children's problems in different ways. This has implications for decisions on intervention and eventual outcome and the potential for a negative effect on a child or young person's self-esteem. We have tried to think about how the client might perceive their problems and emphasised the importance of listening to the voice of the child.

References and further reading

Audit Commission (1998) *Child and Adolescent Mental Health Services*. London, HMSO.

Brammer A (2003) *Social Work Law*. Harlow, Pearson Education.

DoH (1997) *The New NHS: Modern Dependable*. London, HMSO.

DoH (1998) *National Priorities Guidance: Modernising Health and Social Services*. London, HMSO.

DoH (2001) *Framework for the Assessment of Children in Need*. London, HMSO.

HMSO (1981) *The Education Act (1981)*. London, HMSO

HMSO (1983) *The Mental Health Act (1983)*. London, HMSO.

HMSO (1984) *The Data Protection Act (1984)*. London, HMSO.

HMSO (1987) *The Access to Personal Files Act (1987)*. London, HMSO.

HMSO (1989) *The Children Act (1989)*. London, HMSO.

HMSO (1998) *The Crime and Disorder Act (1998)*. London, HMSO.

HMSO (1998) *The Human Rights Act (1998)*. London, HMSO.

HMSO (2001) *The Special Educational Needs and Disability Act (2001)*. London, HMSO.

House of Commons (1997) Child and Adolescent Mental Health Services, Health Committee. London, HMSO.

House of Lords (1985) 3 All E.R. 402, 1985.

Kurtz Z (Ed.) (1992) *With Health in Mind Quality Review Series on Mental Health Care for Children and Young People*. London, Action for Sick Children/NW Thames RHA.

Kurtz Z, Thornes R and Wolkind S (1994) *Services for the Mental Health of Children and Young People in England: A National Review*. London, SW Thames RHA/DoH.

Malek M (1993) *Passing the Buck: Institutional Responses to Children with Difficult Behaviour*. London, Children's Society.

NHS Health Advisory Service (1995) *Together we Stand: Child and Adolescent Mental Health Services*. London, HMSO.

Nixon C and Northrup D (1997) *Evaluating Mental Health Services: How do Programs for Children Work in the Real World?* Thousand Oaks, CA, Sage.

Pearce J (1999) Collaboration Between the NHS and Social Services in the Provision of Child and Adolescent Mental Health Services: A Personal Review. *Child Psychology and Psychiatry Review*. 4: 4, 150-3.

Ryan M (1999) *The Children Act 1989: Putting it Into Practice*. Aldershot, Ashgate.

The Children's Legal Centre (1994) *Mental Health Handbook: A Guide to the Law Affecting Children and Young People*. London, The Children's Legal Centre.

Young Minds (2001) *Briefing on the NSF for Mental Health*. London, Young Minds.

Chapter 5
Planning and intervention

Learning objectives

- Integrate knowledge, skills and values in analysing information and weighing its significance and priority.

- Demonstrate how an assessment leads to a set of concrete objectives for intervention.

- Describe the importance of reflective practice and supervision.

- Identify in partnership with clients the appropriate model and method of intervention that best meets their needs.

Introduction

Every intervention should have a purpose and, as much as possible, that purpose should be identified clearly and openly as part of the agreement established with service users, other key individuals and professionals involved. The seemingly routine task of an assessment interview can be thought of as an intervention in its own right because of the opportunity to gain a greater understanding of young people and their situations in a therapeutic way. That is, by using the opportunity to establish a helping relationship as the basis for initiating change, rather than seeing it as an administrative task.

The choice of intervention open to practitioners in child and adolescent mental health work is necessarily broad because of the wide variety of psychological and social factors influencing the child or young person being helped. Before embarking on any one form of intervention though, you need to reflect on the ethical questions raised by the choices made and the potential consequences. The legal contexts for intervening in children and young people's lives were considered in Chapter 4 and are relevant to this discussion because of the link with consent and competence to understand choices offered.

For example, individual counselling or therapy may succeed in helping a young person to develop a sense of self, but in so doing the experience may alienate them from their family. Family therapy may result in the improvement of a child with emotional difficulties, but in the process of the work siblings may be adversely affected or the parental marriage/partnership exposed as problematic (Sharman, 1997). Even though you may not deliver the work yourself the act of referring to a specialist resource offering specific help means you are sanctioning a potentially powerful intervention in the lives of the child and their family.

You may feel strongly that a child who is bottling up their feelings needs to learn to express them in counselling, but this may cause additional stress to the child who is expected within their community or cultural context, to be developing self-control and containment of emotions. A young person who is displaying destructive obsessional behaviour as a means of managing their stress may be given a behavioural or psychodynamic intervention by a practitioner depending on the particular preference of that individual worker. However, each intervention comes with its own set of assumptions and potential consequences in terms of generating other stressors. The same intervention could be given to two children with the same problem, but only one of them might benefit. These ethical dilemmas are important to acknowledge and reflect upon before proceeding with any course of action. The crucial point is to ensure the most effective intervention is offered for the appropriate problem with the right child.

Activity 5.1

a) You have assessed a young person aged 14 years with a history of drug abuse and depressive illness. There is also a history of parental disharmony and domestic violence. Make a list of the advantages and disadvantages of family therapy.

b) Now put yourself in the place of the young person and see what options appeal most to you.

Preventive practice

The evidence demonstrates conclusively that one of the biggest risk factors in developing adult mental health problems is a history of untreated or inadequately supported childhood mental health problems (DoH, 1998; Howe, 1999; DoH, 2001). Therefore it is imperative that your work addresses this growing problem and offers its own distinctive contribution in the context of preventive practice, and the government's health improvement programme. Early intervention is often synonymous with preventive practice and no more so than in child and adolescent mental health works (Walker, 2001).

The principle of preparing people for potential difficulties is useful and resonates with pro-active initiatives in schools, youth clubs and resources such as telephone helplines/internet discussion groups and campaigns, to reach out to children and young people before they reach a crisis.

One of the most important preventive approaches is helping children and young people cope with the stresses they face in modern society. Every generation has to negotiate the manifestations of stress in their wider culture; therefore relying on ways used by former generations is not useful. This is challenging to practitioners who will naturally draw from their own experiences as an instinctive resource. Therefore the most important starting point first understands the different levels of stress experienced by children and young people. Stress is a broad concept and includes a diverse range of experiences. The key is to ensure that the child themselves can categorise the level of stress. For example, whether bereavement is an acute or moderate stress, or whether parental separation or divorce is a severe and longer-lasting stress. What helps is enabling the child or adolescent to focus on what can be done to improve the situation rather than concentrating on negative feelings (Rutter, 1995).

The Department of Health refocusing children's services initiative, together with the Quality Protects programme, and new Assessment guidance, are all evidence of a policy shift prompted by research into family support services and the limitations of the child protection system designed to influence practitioner education, training, practice, and improve effectiveness (DoH, 1995, 1999, 2000; Thoburn et al., 1998; Statham, 2000). The benefits for preventive, psycho-social work in the area of child and adolescent mental health are likely to be positive. Reducing the likelihood of mental health problems reduces the likelihood of abuse from parents' or carer's inability to cope. Neighbourhood and community projects designed to deter anti-social behaviour and channel youth energies into purposeful activity all have their role to play in CAMHS.

Activity 5.2

a) A pattern of referrals has been noticed in recent months during the warmer weather of children and young people congregating in well-known meeting places for disaffected youth abusing drugs. There are some background issues suggestive of emerging mental health problems. Make a list of the potential stakeholders required to intervene in this situation.

b) How are you going to convince these young people and the other stakeholders of the benefits of participating in any response to this situation?

Empowering practice

Services geared towards the needs of specific age groups of children or young people, or adults, can determine the type of help offered and whether it is perceived as family or individual support (Walker, 2001a). While age is one factor, the type of problem, its degree and duration will also determine where and how help might be offered. Practitioners working in an empowering or participatory way will strive to find, or offer themselves as the most acceptable and accessible type of intervention resource. However, dilemmas will present themselves when parents or children and young people express rigid views about what they want against the best available evidence of what can help.

For example a parent might insist on a child receiving individual counselling to quell troublesome behaviour, whereas all the evidence points towards couple/marital counselling. In specialist settings your offer of help may be rejected because parents insist on a consultation with a psychiatrist – even though this may reinforce their beliefs that their child is the one with the problem. This may inhibit engaging with them in a partnership approach designed to widen their field of vision from scapegoating a child who may be simply displaying the symptoms of familial/marital or environmental causes. These beliefs and perceptions are rooted in a number of factors such as professional status/wanting the best for their child, but they are also driven by deep feelings of guilt, anxiety, fear, and anger. Using a psycho-social model will enable you to respectfully address these in classic congruent, empathic, unconditional positive regard (Rogers, 1951).

The original characteristics of a psycho-social model of work are typically described as understanding the person as well as the problem they are presenting. This means adopting a framework that accepts the notion of the inner and outer worlds of the service user which may be in conflict and result in repetitive, self-destructive behaviour (Woods and Hollis, 1990). While this framework has a strong identification with psycho-dynamic methods of application, it is unhelpful to characterise it as narrow Freudianism or imply it is antipathetic to the needs of black and working class clients. What it does is offer another resource to consider with clients, whether adults or children, whose anxiety, defence mechanisms, and personal difficulties are hampering their attainment of fulfilling relationships with others and hindering effective development. Recognition of the feelings underlying these behaviours offers a rich source of material to work with. Practice based on a psycho-social model therefore (Stepney and Ford, 2000):

- Concentrates on the present rather than the past.

- Attempts to help people achieve equilibrium between their inner emotional states and the pressures they face in the outside world.

- Uses the service user's relationship with the practitioner actively.

However, a modern psycho-social model requires refinement to take account of the need for emphasis on culturally competent, empowering, and community-oriented practice. Eurocentric assumptions about normative standards of behaviour against which to assess psychological functioning have been criticised as dismissive of black and other ethnic minority constructions of self-identity and development (Robinson, 1995). These criticisms can be applied to any model of practice that relies on stereotyped, one-dimensional assessment. The advantage of such a refined model is both the explicit inclusivity and the importance of an examination of feelings generated during the helping process. Table 5.1 is based on the strengths and difficulties questionnaire designed by Professor Robert Goodman as a tool for practitioners. This can be downloaded from www.youthinmind.net free and adapted for work with children and parents in beginning the process of work (Goodman, 1997).

Reflective practice is considered to be the hallmark of modern practice among professionals working with people in a helping role. It has resonance with the ideas contained in psycho-dynamic skills of practitioner self-awareness and the feelings generated in the helping relationship between worker and service user. It is recommended as a way of evaluating the impact of intervention and done in partnership can be empowering for some clients. Supervision or professional consultation in the area of child and adolescent mental health is a crucial component of reflective practice. A manager with the skills to offer case consultation combined with management supervision is ideal but probably a rarity.

Table 5.1: Strengths and difficulties questionnaire

	Not true	Somewhat true	Certainly true
Considerate of other peoples feelings			
Restless, overactive, cannot stay still for long			
Often complains of headaches, stomach-aches			
Shares readily with other children			
Often has temper tantrums or hot tempers			
Rather solitary, tends to play alone			
Generally obedient, usually does what adults ask			
Many worries, often seems worried			
Helpful if someone is hurt, upset or feeling ill			
Has at least one good friend			
Constantly fidgeting or squirming			
Often fights with other children or bullies them			
Often unhappy, down-hearted or tearful			
Generally liked by other children			
Easily distracted, concentration wanders			
Nervous or clingy in new situations, easily loses confidence			
Kind to younger children			
Often lies or cheats			
Picked on or bullied by other children			
Often volunteers to help others			
Thinks things out before acting			
Steals from home, school or elsewhere			
Gets on better with adults than other children			
Many fears, easily scared			
Sees tasks through to the end, good attention span			

Goodman, 1997.

Practitioners involved with families or in situations where child mental health problems are an issue require quality consultation separate from the administrative and managerial aspects of their work. A senior colleague or other professional might be the best resource as long as they can help you disentangle your own feelings from those being generated during intense work. Simple concepts such as transference and projection used in a pragmatic way can go a long way towards increasing effectiveness and clarity in confusing and worrying situations.

Activity 5.3

a) You have been working individually with a female child aged 9 for three months on a weekly basis, following a period of school refusal/phobia. The child is now happier, less anxious and sociable but adamant she is not returning to school. The multi-agency professionals involved are split on how to proceed.

b) How do you make sense of this situation and what theoretical and practical resources can help you?

Analysing and planning

In developing a deeper understanding of difficulties with a view to deciding on intervention, you can draw on a range of theories and methods. Differing hypotheses result from viewing situations with the aid of these theories. This is healthy although it can be unhelpful if it leads to confusion and drift in your practice. At its best it can help guard against the temptation to claim a single truth in any situation. Forming alternative understandings and explanations is a good habit to acquire. However, judgements have to be made and will be demanded by managers and expected in legal proceedings where they will be examined and tested. The most desirable practice is where an interpretation is helpful to both you and your client in developing solutions, and where it is rooted in values of respect and anti-oppressive practice.

Maintaining a reflexive stance helps you consider the consequences of using particular theories and encouraging service users to develop their own theories about their situations. You will need more than one model of assessment and intervention to enable you to meet the needs of all your clients – if not you will be like a plumber with only one spanner. Having a grasp of different models of practice should enable you, with the client, to select the most appropriate, and help you maintain a degree of open-mindedness. This process will enable you to plan your intervention by integrating and analysing information and forming a judgement in partnership with your client.

Integrating knowledge, skills and values in analysing information and being able to weigh its significance and priority as a basis for effective planning is a demanding task. O'Sullivan (1999) suggests that sound planning will happen provided the following elements in the decision-making process are delineated:

- **Being critically aware of and taking into account the decision making contexts:** Knowledge of legal requirements and agency procedures are critical ingredients of planning what is possible and permissible. Statutory duty has to be balanced against your endeavour to take a holistic perspective of the situation.

- **Involving the client to the highest feasible level:** There can be four levels – being told; being consulted; being a partner; and being in control. A key skill is to fit the level of involvement to the nature of the particular planning situation.

- **Consulting with all stakeholders:** There could be numerous stakeholders involved in your work with a particular service user. Some will have more systematic contact but only general knowledge about the client, but they could be just as valuable as someone with limited contact but who has specialised knowledge. A range of perceptions can either enhance the clarity in a situation or confirm your hypothesis, or produce a disparate and confusing picture, which hinders rather than helps.

- **Being clear in your thinking and aware of your emotions:** A heightened element of self-awareness is always useful. Over-reacting to a situation on the basis of tiredness, stress, and the day of the week or simply false information needs to be guarded against. Equally, under-reacting to a risky situation because of feelings of pity, empathy, or over-optimism can contribute to an escalation of risk factors.

- **Producing a well-reasoned frame of the decision situation that is consistent with the available information:** Through framing processes you can shape the information into a picture of the situation, planning goals and a set of options. Listing key factors and considering the weight to give to each requires knowledge, experience, and the capacity for short and long-term predictions of the consequences of various interventions.

- **Basing your course of action on a systematic appraisal of the options:** The plan could be based on the principle that a statutory duty overrides the traumatic impact of the subsequent intervention. Or which option is likely to provide the best outcome in the context of risk assessment and available supportive resources.

Strategies for integration

Learning arises as a result of the four-stage process of concrete experience; reflective observation; abstract conceptualisation; and active experimentation. You can use this model to describe and facilitate the application of your knowledge and theory to practice. The following points can guide you in this process (Thompson, 2002):

- Guard against the false belief in theoryless practice.

- Research-minded practice can help integrate theory and practice.

- The critical incident technique is a way of analysing a situation where strong emotions were raised in your practice and which interfered with your ability to function effectively then or could in future.

- Developing a group approach for narrowing the gap between theory and practice can be very effective.

- Planning intervention in your work and the decision-making process includes thinking and feeling about the situation being addressed.

In health and social care practice there are professionals who testify to the efficacy of intuitive practice or practice wisdom gleaned from years of experience. Others frown on this notion and subscribe to the concept of objectivity and the value of methodological rigour offered by clear analysis of all the factors in a situation. As with many polarised debates the desire to simplify in order to heighten differences can obscure the valuable resources within each approach. It needs to be acknowledged that analysis is not inevitably technical, that intuition can be unreliable, but both can offer you equally useful ways of thinking.

Intuition

Intuition has been variously described as the absence of analysis, the pinnacle of expertise, or the unconscious processing of data. This means that the basis for the consequent judgement is not made explicit at the time. It can be thought of as deciding in a relatively holistic way, without separating the decision situation into its various elements. This enables it to be a quick way of deciding by making use of limited information by sensing patterns and filling in gaps. To be reliable and accurate, intuition needs to be based on expertise developed over time, but it has a fundamental drawback which stems from its implicit nature. This is that the reasons behind intuitive decisions are not readily available for comment and scrutiny, which is necessary for partnership practice.

Analysis

Analysis can be defined as a step by step, conscious, logically defensible process. There is deliberation over the different elements in a situation in a systematic and organised way. It can be thought of as using selected information in a precise way, whereas intuition uses all of the perceived information in an imprecise way. The strength of analysis is that it encourages openness about reasoning and so potentially holds your work open to scrutiny. The disadvantage in this approach is that it can induce misplaced faith in the ability to make predictions particularly in the increasing field of risk assessment.

Synthesis

Seeing intuition and analysis as opposites can obscure the potential compatibility and complementarily of the approaches. Some planning decisions will require breaking down into their component parts and given careful consideration. But because this involves issues of uncertainty and values, intuition needs to be used within analysis in the making of judgements about the significance of information. Combining the explicitness of analysis with the skilled judgements of professional intuition offers you the advantages of each approach. When facilitating client decision making or making decisions in partnership, some degree of analysis will be helpful as it involves being explicit about the basis of choice.

Activity 5.4

a) Spend ten minutes thinking about the constraints on planning intervention in child and adolescent mental health work.

b) Discuss your findings with a colleague or supervisor and consider the strategies you might use for managing.

Methods and models of practice

The following methods and models of practice are not unique to CAMHS work nor are they an exclusive list. They have been chosen from the range of modern methods and models available to aid clarity in selection of the most appropriate components of an effective intervention in child and adolescent mental health work (Payne, 1997; Milner and O'Byrne, 1998; Stepney and Ford, 2000; Dogra et al., 2002). Discussion of the merits of defining methods and models of practice has been avoided for reasons of space, while the issue of efficacy is discussed in the final chapter.

Crisis intervention

Work with any client group in a variety of agency contexts will sooner or later expose you to a crisis of some form or another. Crisis intervention has become a practice with a theoretical base and can be identified by certain characteristics. Crisis theory is described as a time when a person finds themselves much more dependent on external sources of support than at other times in their life. It has been described as having three distinct phases (Caplan, 1964):

- **Impact** – recognising a threat.

- **Recoil** – attempting to restore equilibrium but failing leaving the person feeling stressed and defeated.

- **Adjustment/adaptation or breakdown** – when the person begins to move to a different level of functioning.

It is usually interrelated factors and triggers that produce a state of crisis, some of which can be anticipated while others cannot. Another concept to help understand what crisis means is that it is a stage of disequilibrium when tension and anxiety have risen to a peak and the individual's built in devices no longer operate (Golan, 1969). Rather than see crises as failures of individuals or systems it is useful to think of them as opportunities for significant interventions at times when stakeholders are more likely to engage with your strategy.

Characteristics

- Crisis intervention employs ideas from psychodynamic theory in understanding the way each person can be helped to gain insight into their functioning and discover ways of coping better.

- Used in conjunction with risk assessment and risk management techniques.

- Short-term in nature.

- Crisis intervention relates a client's internal crises to external changes.

- It can help in cases of bereavement, loss, reactive depression, trauma.

- Based on the notion that people can return to previous level of functioning depending on the nature of the problem, and the quality of help provided.

Systemic practice

Employing a systemic or systems model in child and adolescent mental health practice will be characterised by the key notion that individual children and young people have a social context which will be influencing to a greater or lesser extent, their behaviour and their perception of their problem. An important social context is that of the family and this has led to the practice of family therapy as a method of practice. It offers a broad framework for intervention enabling the mapping of all the important elements affecting families as well as a method of working with those elements to effect beneficial change. Key features include:

- Convening family meetings to give voice to everyone connected to an individual's problem (e.g. family group conference).

- Constructing a geneogram (family tree) with a family to help identify the quality of relationships.

- Harnessing the strengths of families to support individuals in trouble.

- Using a problem-oriented style to energise the family to find their own solutions.

- Assisting in the development of insight into patterns of behaviour and communication within the family system.

- Adopting a neutral position as far as possible in order to avoid accusations of bias/collusion.

Many professionals use this model as an overarching framework to help guide their practice. It is particularly useful to use to clarify situations where there is multi-agency and multi-professional involvement in client's lives. It can help the drawing of boundaries and sort out who does what in often complex, fast-moving, and confusing situations. It also helps avoid the assumption that the individual child or young person is necessarily the main focus for intervention.

Disadvantages

It can be difficult for some families to appreciate the interconnectedness of the problems of individual children with wider influences. It is a way of viewing the position, role and behaviour of various individuals within the context of the whole system, but in so doing appear abstract, culturally insensitive, and disempowering. Used uncritically it can negate the importance of individual work, as well as avoiding location of responsibility in child abuse situations.

Psychodynamic practice

The model offers a concept of the mind, its mechanisms, and a method of understanding why some children behave in seemingly repetitive, destructive ways. It is the essential one to one helping relationship involving advanced listening and communication skills. It provides a framework to address profound disturbances and inner conflicts within children and adolescents around issues of loss, attachment, anxiety, and personal development. Key ideas such as defence mechanisms, and the transference in the relationship between worker and client, can be extremely helpful in reviewing the work being undertaken, and in the process of supervision. The model helps evaluate the strong feelings aroused in particular work situations, where for example a client transfers feelings and attitudes onto the worker that derive from an earlier significant relationship. Counter-transference occurs when you try to live up to that expectation and behave for example, like the client's parent. Key features include:

- It is a useful way of attempting to understand seemingly irrational behaviour.

- The notion of defence mechanisms is a helpful way of assessing male adolescents who have difficulty expressing their emotions.

- It acknowledges the influence of past events/attachments and can create a healthy suspicion about surface behaviour.

- The development of insight can be a particularly empowering experience to enable children and young people to understand themselves and take more control over their own lives.

- The model has influenced a listening, accepting approach that avoids over-directiveness.

- It can be used to assess which developmental stage is reflected in the child or young person's behaviour and to gauge the level of anxiety/depression.

Disadvantages

The conventional criticisms of this model are its genesis in a medical model of human behaviour that relies on expert opinion without too much account of the person in their socio-economic context. In its original, uncritical form it pathologies homosexuality and negates gender power relationships. It is not considered an appropriate way of working with some ethnic minority groups and on its own cannot adequately explain the effects of racism.

Behavioural practice

Practice with this model is based on the key concept that all behaviour is learned and therefore available to be unlearned or changed. It offers a framework for assessing the pattern of behaviour in children and adolescents and a method for altering their thinking, feeling, and behaviour. The intervention can be used with individuals and groups of young people. It aims to help them become aware of themselves, link thoughts and emotions, and enable them to acquire new life skills. Using this approach you would decide on the goals/new behaviours to be achieved with the client, those that are clear but also capable of measurement.

Key features include:

- Using the ABC formula – what are the **A**ntecedents, the **B**ehaviour and the **C**onsequences of the problem.

- Focusing on what behaviours are desired and reinforcing them.

- Modelling and rehearsing desired behavioural patterns.

- Combining behavioural and cognitive approaches to produce better results.

- Gradually desensitising a child or young person to a threat or phobia.

Behavioural approaches have appeal for staff undertaking intervention because it offers a systematic, scientific approach from which to structure their practice. The approach goes some way towards encouraging participatory practice, discouraging labelling, and maintains the client's story as central. The idea of learned helplessness has the potential to bridge the gap between psychological and sociological explanations of behaviour, maintaining the focus on both social and individual factors.

Disadvantages

Usually it is only the immediate environment of the child that is examined. It is not as value-free as it claims. The scientific nature of behavioural assessment rests on modernist assumptions about certainty. There is often in practice a tendency to rush a solution after a limited assessment where the theory is bent so that the individual client changes to accommodate their circumstances rather than the other way round. The potential to use the theory to employ anti-oppressive practice is limited because much of the theory is based on white, male, western norms of behaviour.

Task centred practice

Task centred work is often cited as the most popular base for contemporary assessment and intervention practice, but it may be that it is used as a set of activities rather than as a theoretically-based approach from which a set of activities flows. Key features include:

- It is based on client agreement or service user acceptance of a legal justification for action.
- It aims to move from problem to goal, from what is wrong to what is needed.
- It is based around tasks which are central to the process of change and which aim to build on individual service user strengths as far as possible.
- The approach is time-limited, preserving client self-esteem and independence as far as possible.
- It is a highly structured model of practice using a building block approach so that each task can be agreed and success or not measured by moving from problem to goal.

It can serve as a basic approach for the majority of children and young people. In this approach the problem is always the problem as defined by the client. It therefore respects their values, beliefs and perceptions. This approach encourages children and young people to select the problem they want to work on and engages them in task selection and review. It lends itself to a collaborative and empowering approach by enabling you to carry out your share of tasks and review them alongside the clients. Time limits and task reviews aid motivation and promote optimism.

Disadvantages

Although this approach has the capacity for empowerment, it can sometimes prohibit active measures by practitioners to ensure it does. Although ostensibly value-free and intrinsically non-oppressive, you should continually reflect on your practice to make this explicit. The coaching role could be open to abuse, or permit you to become overly directive. The emphasis on simple, measurable tasks may focus attention on concrete solutions that obscure the potential advocacy role of practice. The approach requires a degree of cognitive ability and motivation in the child or young person that in some cases will be lacking.

■ LEARNING REVIEW

We have thought about the dilemmas in planning intervention in CAMHS work particularly with regard to the potential consequences of any chosen intervention on a child and their wider social context. The legal and agency responsibilities governing your practice may conflict with your desire for working in partnership with the child or young person of concern.

The elements of preventive and empowering practice have been reviewed and the importance of early intervention highlighted. Government and agency policy guidance is now geared to providing resources to enable you to participate in preventive activity to stop the deterioration in the mental health of vulnerable children and young people.

The importance of analysis and planning intervention based on the best possible evidence from a wide range of sources has been underlined. The potential conflict between intuitive and analytic practice can be seen as a false dichotomy in that elements of both offer the optimum way forward when weighing up the assessment information. Combining the explicitness of analysis with the skilled judgements of professional intuition offers you the advantages of each approach.

A representative selection of common methods and models of intervention able to be used by qualified professionals in health and social care have been described. Their advantages and disadvantages have been reviewed in order to offer you choices that fit with your preferred style of working and to gain some understanding of the principles of other interventions.

References and further reading

Caplan G (1964) *Principles of Preventive Psychiatry*. London, Basic Books.

Dallos R and Draper R (2000) *An Introduction to Family Therapy*. Buckingham, OU Press.

Dogra N, Parkin A, Gale F and Frake C (2002) *A Multidisciplinary Handbook of Child and Adolescent Mental Health for Front-line Professionals*. London, Jessica Kingsley.

DoH (1995) *A Handbook on Child and Adolescent Mental Health*. London, HMSO.

DoH (1998) *Modernising Mental Health Services: Safe, Supportive and Sensible*. London, HMSO.

DoH (2000) *Framework for the Assessment of Children in Need.* London, HMSO.

DoH (2000) *National Service Framework for Mental Health.* London, HMSO.

DoH (2000) *Social Services Inspectorate: Excellence not Excuses: Inspection of Services for Ethnic Minority Children and Families.* London, HMSO.

DoH (2001) *Children Looked After in England:2000/2001.* London, HMSO.

Goodman R (1997) The strengths and difficulties questionnaire: a research note. *Journal of Child Psychology and Psychiatry.* 38: 5, 581-6.

Hill M (1999). *Effective Ways of Working With Children and Their Families.* London, Jessica Kingsley.

Howe D (Ed.) (1999) *Attachment and Loss in Child and Family Social Work.* Aldershot, Ashgate.

Milner J and O'Byrne P (1998) *Assessment in Social Work Practice.* London, Macmillan.

O'Sullivan T (1999) *Decision Making in Social Work.* London, Macmillan.

Payne M (1997) *Modern Social Work Theory.* London, Macmillan.

Robinson L (1995) *Psychology for Social Workers: Black Perspectives.* London, Routledge.

Rogers C (1951) *Client-centred Therapy.* Boston, MA, Houghton Mifflin.

Rutter M and Smith D (1995) *Psychosocial Disorders in Young People.* London, Wiley.

Sharman W (1997) *Children and Adolescents With Mental Health Problems.* London, Bailliere Tindall.

Statham J (2000) *Outcomes and Effectiveness of Family Support Services: A Research Review.* London, Institute for Education, University of London.

Stepney R and Ford S (2000) *Social Work Models, Methods, and Theories.* Lyme Regis, Russell House.

Sutton C (2000) *Child and Adolescent Behaviour Problems.* Leicester, BPS.

Thoburn J, Wilding J and Watson J (1998) *Children in Need: A Review of Family Support Work in Three Local Authorities.* Norwich, University of East Anglia/DoH.

Thompson N (2002) *Building the Future – Social Work with Children, Young People and Their Families.* Lyme Regis, Russell House Publishing.

Walker S (2001a) Developing Child and Adolescent Mental Health Services. *Journal of Child Health Care.* 5: 2, 71-6.

Walker S (2001b) Consulting with Children and Young People. *The International Journal of Children's Rights.* 9: 45-56.

Woods M and Hollis F (1990) *Casework: A Psychological Process.* 2nd edn. New York, Random House.

Chapter 6
Effectiveness and evaluation

Learning objectives

- Explain why practice should be evidence based.

- Identify methods of practice evaluation.

- Involve clients in evaluation using a children's rights perspective.

- Explain how evaluation can contribute to the effective planning and management of CAMHS at both practice and agency levels.

Introduction

There is as yet no substantial evidence base for effectiveness in services for children and adolescents with mental health problems. One of the few contemporary attempts to collate the available methodologically robust research emphasises the importance of specifying what intervention works for which families with what problems (Carr, 2000).

This is not an easy task. Evaluating provision in child and adolescent mental health services is particularly challenging because of the difficulty in isolating any factor which can be clearly demonstrated to have affected outcome (Target and Fonagy, 1996; Hunter et al., 1996; Audit Commission, 1999). The wide range of professionals from many agencies having some impact on child mental health is so diverse as to make it unrealistic to identify a linear sequence of causality from intervention through to outcome. There are just so many informal, psychosocial influences affecting children's emotional and behavioural development in the short-term or cumulatively over the long-term. Table 6.1 provides a guide to enable you to consider the range of approaches for particular problems. These are intended as a broad guide only bearing in mind that every individual child requires support that feels right for them in their unique circumstances.

Table 6.1: Mental health problems and possible interventions

Mental health problem	Intervention
Anorexia/bulimia nervosa	Family therapy, Psychotherapy, Cognitive-behaviour therapy
Anxiety	Counselling, School based group work, Behaviour therapy, Family therapy
Enuresis/encopresis	Behaviour therapy
School refusal	Behaviour therapy
Obsessional disorder	Medication, Cognitive-behaviour therapy
Reading difficulties	Psychotherapy, Counselling
Depression/grief	Psychotherapy, Counselling, Cognitive-behaviour therapy, Family therapy
Diabetes control	Psychotherapy, Counselling
Child abuse	Individual or group therapy, Parent training
Conduct disorder/aggression	Cognitive-behaviour therapy, Family therapy, Parent training, Foster care
ADHD	Social skills training, Family Therapy, Parent training, Behaviour therapy, Medication
Adjustment to divorce/separation	Counselling, Problem-solving training, Social skills training
Oppositional defiant disorder	Parent training, Behaviour therapy, Group work, Problem-solving training
Drug abuse	Family therapy, Problem solving training, Social skills training

Graham, 1996; Child Psychotherapy Trust, 1998; Carr, 2000; McNeish et al., 2002.

Effectiveness studies have tended to neglect the views of service users and especially children as independent evaluators (Sanford et al., 1992; Kent and Read, 1998; Laws et al., 1999). Equally, in studies attempting to validate service user evaluation a trend towards positive bias has been identified particularly where treatment is continuing (Polowczyk, 1993). In seeking to measure or gauge the impact of your work with children and adolescents in the area of mental health you face a difficult challenge particularly in the context of the drive to evidence-based practice. Traditional scientific research based methods are beyond the capacity of practitioners who are just about managing their caseloads and the day-to-day administration involved. The traditional randomised control trial may not provide a comprehensive assessment of outcome or represent accurately what actually happens in practice (Barnes et al., 1997; Barton, 1999). However, you can incorporate the concepts of effectiveness and evaluation in ways consistent with your professional ethics and values and in the best interests of their clients and by adopting a children's rights perspective.

Activity 6.1

a) Together with a colleague discuss your agency's policy and procedures for evaluating practice.

b) How does this information inform the practice of individual practitioners?

The practice evidence-base

Central to an empowering socially inclusive approach in work with children and adolescents is finding out whether the work has contributed towards the process of change and the practice evidence base. Change can be considered as something that is endless, constant and inevitable. How it is perceived and experienced by service users is crucial. Various models of intervention examined in Chapter 5 permit changes stemming from within the psyche of the person to physical changes in their environment and abilities. There are changes imposed on certain clients compulsorily and those that are accepted voluntarily – either of which may lead to long-term benefits for them or their kin. Change is often thought of as something initiated by a practitioner in a linear cause and effect process. But it can be useful to think about it in a more circular or reflexive pattern. How much did you change during the course of an intervention? What impact did the client have on you and how did this affect your thinking and behaviour? Indeed, most of the change may occur within yourself as you find out more over time about a child and their circumstances compared to the first encounter.

Change is connected to difference but every stakeholder in the change process has a unique perception of what counts as difference. Pointing out differences to a child or adolescent might be experienced as empowering but it might equally provoke feelings of fear or anxiety. A minimum amount of help might produce significant changes and equally a substantial amount of intervention results in no change or a worsening of circumstances. Where you choose to look for change may not be where other professionals or the service user is looking. Change can therefore be liberating or constraining, it can generate enlightenment or promote feelings of anger, loss and bereavement. Maintaining a degree of professional optimism with realism and managing uncertainty with a modest and respectful approach offers you the potential for being a useful resource to your clients.

Seven stages of change have been described which serve as a useful tool for practitioners trying to evaluate their practice and assess the effectiveness of the chosen intervention with an individual child or young person (Rogers, 1957). The stages can be used with the child or young person, or parent/carer, to include them in the process of insight, personal development and self-reflection:

Stage 1: Communication is about external events.

Stage 2: Expression flows more freely.

Stage 3: Describes personal reactions to external events.

Stage 4: Descriptions of feelings and personal experiences.

Stage 5: Present feelings are expressed.

Stage 6: A flow of feeling which has a life of its own.

Stage 7: A series of felt senses connecting different aspects of an issue.

The need to expand and refine the evidence base of CAMHS practice in order to demonstrate effectiveness is more important than ever. The growing problem requires a concerted effort from all agencies in contact with children and young people to understand the services they are providing and finding out better ways of measuring success. Three key factors have been identified in defining and explaining why evidence-based practice is not an option, but a necessity (Sheldon and Chilvers, 2000):

Conscientiousness – this means a constant vigilance to monitor and review your practice and to maintain service user welfare as paramount. It entails keeping up to date with new developments and a commitment to further professional understanding of human growth and development and social problems.

Explicitness – this means working in an open and honest way with clients based on reliable evidence of what works and what is understood to be effective. The principle of explicitness demands a review of the available options with clients based upon thorough assessment of their problems.

Judiciousness – this means the exercise of sound, prudent, sensible judgement. Potential risks arising from some, or no intervention either in cases or policies, should be thoroughly assessed and evaluated in the knowledge that not all eventualities can be predicted.

The drive to encourage research-minded professionalism in order to improve practice standards and accountability is, however, in danger of producing a confusion of research studies varying in quality and methodological rigour yet producing potentially useful data hidden within the quantity being produced. Practitioner research is being encouraged as a means of influencing policy, management and practice using evaluative concepts moulded by service-user expectations. In the context of child and adolescent mental health you can contribute to good quality effectiveness and evaluation studies by working in partnership with children and young people to ensure their perspectives are at the heart of this activity. Quantitative measures that examine changes in symptoms that caused the initial concern are commonly used to evaluate outcome in child and adolescent mental health services. A particular set of measures is now being put into practice that was originally designed for adult mental health (Gowers et al., 1999; Gowers et al., 2000). Table 6.2 illustrates how the items measured are classified into sections and a severity index is calculated for before and after comparison.

Table 6.2: Health of the Nation Outcome Scales (HoNOSCA)

Scale item	Section
Disruptive/aggressive behaviour	**Behaviour**
Overactivity and attentional difficulty	
Non-accidental self-injury	
Alcohol, substance/solvent misuse	
Scholastic or language skills	**Impairment**
Physical illness/disability problems	
Hallucinations and delusions	
Non-organic and somatic symptoms	
Emotional and related symptoms	
Peer relationships	**Social**
Self-care and relationships	
Family life and relationships	
Poor school attendance	
Lack of knowledge-nature of difficulties	**Information**
Lack of information-services/management	
(each scale item scored in range 0-4)	

Gowers et al., 2000.

Children and young people as service evaluators

Effectiveness and evaluation in child and adolescent mental health services has tended to be a service or professional-led enterprise. Managers and practitioners have developed methods and models of evaluating service provision using sophisticated research designs, methodologies, and computerised analysis to try to tell them something useful about the process and outcomes of their work. These can range from huge epidemiological studies to try to assess likely demand for certain services, through to micro studies of small organisational operations contemplating changes. The majority of these studies tend to be quantitative designs linked to clinical audit where service use is calculated against cost and efficiency measures such as length of client contact time. Evaluation is defined as making an assessment of the merit of an activity or intervention and measuring it against the goals that were established at the outset (Barlow et al., 2001). Quantitative approaches have been unfavourably compared to qualitative approaches because they lack the intensity, subtlety, particularity, ethical judgement and relevance required for example, by social workers (Shaw, 1999; May, 2002).

Children's perspectives and the qualitative information that articulates their agenda have rarely been explored in relation to the help they receive towards their emotional and mental wellbeing (Hill, 1999; Gordon and Grant, 1997). Findings that young people with mental health problems are reluctant to make use of specialist services or quickly cease contact indicates the importance of developing appropriate local sources of help (Mental Health Foundation, 1999; Audit Commission, 1999; Richardson and Joughin, 2000). It is crucial that children and young people are properly consulted to ensure that provision is experienced as useful and relevant and therefore going to be used effectively. In order to do that methods of consulting with children and young people need to be developed that are appropriate, effective and methodologically robust (Walker, 2001).

Several studies provide some evidence of the effectiveness of attempts to ascertain the perceptions of children and young people about services they have received. There is among some practitioners and researchers a general assumption that seeking the views of children and young people is of itself a good thing. Yet the purpose of gaining such perceptions can be varied, the methods employed quite different, and the evidence of the impact of seeking their views, obscure. A meta-review of these studies concluded that with the increasing interest in seeking children's views there need to be better developed instruments for measuring satisfaction and gaining children's evaluation of the services they receive (Hennessey, 1999). Research on children's evaluations of education, paediatrics, and child mental health services was assessed. Only a minority of studies examined had presented information on the structure, reliability, and validity of the instruments they used.

The extent to which children's evaluations are similar to the evaluations of parents raises important questions about validity. It can be assumed that perceptions should be different, but in the area of child and adolescent mental health differences in perception of the help received can indicate that the underlying cause of the difficulty remains untreated. The parents who want a child to conform and change their behaviour will have a different view from that of the child, who wants them to stop arguing and fighting. In the case of a child this can result in symptom deterioration reinforcing parental perceptions that it is the child who has the problem. Such a consequence could lead to disillusionment and produce a resistance from the child at an older age to engaging with further help, thereby contributing to the development of mental health problems into adulthood.

It is important to explore the extent to which services are meeting the needs of differing groups of children in terms of age, gender, ethnicity, religion, and socio-economic status. The research on the relationship between client satisfactions in mental health services is better developed than in any other service sector. Three types of outcome have been used: client-assessed, parent-assessed, and therapist-assessed. There are inconsistent findings reported for the relationship between client satisfaction and therapist evaluation of treatment progress. The problem of practitioner power and status is regarded as influential in determining the ability of children and young people to express discontent with help offered. It is recognised that children and young people feel under pressure to say what they expect the practitioner to hear. In this context you need to call upon your relationship-building skills and create an atmosphere of honesty and trust in order to obtain authentic feedback.

A few studies have looked at the relationship with personal and/or family variables. Understanding these relationships is potentially important for understanding the way in which services may or may not be meeting the needs of various clients. The information currently available is limited. There have been relatively small numbers of attempts to do this and those that have, used different measures. It is now acknowledged at central government level that children from different socio-economic backgrounds may have differential access to mental health services and/or different expectations from services, but to date these possibilities have not been further explored (Audit Commission, 1999).

Age is a particularly important variable because of the different cognitive, social and emotional needs and abilities of children of different ages. Although individual studies differed in whether younger or older clients were more satisfied, a sufficient number of studies reported a moderate or high correlation between age and satisfaction or dissatisfaction. Only a small number of studies explored the relationship between gender and satisfaction but the evidence suggests no general tendency for greater satisfaction to be associated with either boys or girls. A more useful approach may be to explore the relationship between client/staff gender combinations (Bernzweig et al., 1997).

There is very little evidence in many studies to demonstrate what impact their findings had on service development or practitioner attitudes and skills. A shift in thinking is required from perceiving children and young people as recipients of health promotion efforts on their behalf, to accepting children and young people as active participants in the whole process. Another gap in the literature is the limited information on how children and young people felt about being asked their views on the service that they had received. Some children may feel perturbed by this while others are enthusiastic about being given the opportunity to be part of a reflective process. It is a reasonable assumption that in the case of children and young people with mental health problems, those keenest to contribute are likely to reflect a positive perception of the service whereas those least keen reflect a negative experience. It is important for practitioners and researchers to continue to develop creative and flexible methods for enabling representative contributions from all those receiving the same service.

Activity 6.2

a) Spend a little time reflecting on a recent period of work and the way cases were assessed for effectiveness.

b) Now consider how the reviews/summaries/conclusions could be collated to inform future practice changes.

Children's and young people's experiences of help

Practitioners have built up a repertoire of therapeutic methods in working with children and young people, engaging with them in areas of great sensitivity such as bereavement, parental separation, or sexual abuse. The same repertoire of research techniques is yet to be developed to ensure that children and young people are being given the best possible chance of contributing to service evaluation. Few studies have been undertaken with regard to therapeutic interventions with children and young people experiencing emotional and behavioural difficulties and whether they found the therapy helpful. Those undertaken have found generally children speak less than parents when interviewed together. Adolescents express themselves in limited ways tending to agree/disagree; while therapists spoke more often to parents than to children when attempting to evaluate the help and support offered (Marshal et al., 1989, Mas et al., 1985; Cederborg, 1997). The question is whether this reflects a generalisable aversion from children to participating in research of this nature or whether the research design militates against inclusion and active participation.

Children's reactions to therapy can be influenced by their attachment style. In families where there are insecure attachments for example, children can feel constrained to speak more freely because of fears of what the consequences might be and the discomfort in exposing painful or difficult feelings (Smith et al., 1996; Strickland-Clark et al., 2000). This poses important challenges for practitioners and researchers wanting to gain feedback from children and young people with mental health problems where there are factors likely to inhibit participation. The alternative is to automatically exclude some children and young people and miss the opportunity to gather valuable evidence to improve service provision rather than designing strategies to overcome these difficulties. Ways to engage such children have been developed and could be adapted by researchers.

There is little guidance available in the research literature about conversational methods with children. Even child psychology texts concentrate on experimental, observational and standard measurement techniques (Vasta, Haith and Miller, 1993). The perceived power and status of adults affect children in interview situations and by presumptions about what answers are expected. The combination of adult assumptions about children and young persons' competence in contributing to service evaluation, together with children and young persons' assumptions about adult power and authority, conspire to hinder meaningful developments to improve the situation.

Methodologies for including children

When efforts are made to overcome resistance to incorporating children and young persons' perceptions in service evaluation there is much evidence of creative and sensitive work being undertaken (Walker, 2001b). Several studies conclude that there are a number of factors that can help a practitioner in gaining confidence and the co-operation of young people, together with their perceptions and views (Finch, 1987; Pollard, 1987; Hill et al., 1996; Hazel, 1995). These are summarised below:

- **The fieldwork setting:** needs to achieve a balance between privacy needed for confidential data collection, and openness to public scrutiny for assuring the personal safety of the young person and minimise any risk of allegations of impropriety against the practitioner.

- **Vignettes:** of relevant social situations presented to a group of children for comment may be a particularly useful tool to use at the beginning of an interview to break the ice and encourage someone other than the practitioner to speak.

- **Short stories:** containing issues that might draw strong moral opinions, are likely to produce more confident information flow.

- **Pictures and photographs:** are effective ways of obtaining the full attention of young participants, demanding concentration of the eyes and mind. Having an object to handle can also be reassuring.

- **Free imagination and play:** young participants seem more enthusiastic and confident about telling their versions of events rather than commenting on vignettes created by the researcher. This encourages and corresponds to developmental level requiring characters or figures from their own sex.

- **Quotations or catch-phrases:** can be useful in encouraging strong opinions from children, these can be proverbs, or common sayings such as 'children should be seen and not heard'. Linked with popular culture drawn from media, especially TV soaps and news events, presentation of this material can provide successful sources of stimulation.

- **Problem solving:** children seem to draw comfort from their own knowledge and common ground held by the practitioner. Asking young people to propose a solution to a practical problem enables them to deal with problems involved in caring for people of their own or a younger age and enables the researcher to explore the reasons and more abstract beliefs behind the chosen solution. Presenting a problem in the style of a teenage magazine problem page may be a very accessible way of developing this technique.

It is important to continually reassure participants that there are no correct or incorrect responses to any issues that arise. Fear of false perceptions may be more likely in an educational setting where tests are a familiar occurrence. A mixture of focus group and individual interview techniques with children and adolescents on the subject of emotional and behavioural difficulties demonstrates an effective combination (Hill et al., 1996). Focus group discussions have acquired prominence in recent years and their use with children can result in more information generated by individuals who are encouraged to voice their opinions when others do so. They seem able to develop their own points in response to the stimulation, challenge, and memory-prompting of what others say. There are individuals who do not find this format helpful, and it is important for the interviewer to facilitate productive peer interaction rather than create many individual interviews happening at the same time.

The optimum size of the group is recommended to be five to six, with a small age range, while some advocate single-sex groups (Greenbaum, 1987; Triseliotis et al., 1995). It may be that gender differences at specific developmental stages can serve to accentuate different styles of expression, therefore thought needs to be put in to consider the optimum age range and gender mix of children. Another area with the potential to provide a rich source of information is in non-verbal communication. The advantage of developing methodologies for interpreting this level of communication is that it can enable access to much younger children's perceptions and those with disabilities, sensory impairments or developmental delays.

Ethics and children's rights

There is a growing literature on the subject of the rights of children and young people to influence decisions about their own health and healthcare (MacFarlane and McPherson, 1995; Treseder, 1997; Wilson, 1999; Alderson, 2000). Parents and those with parental responsibility might present powerful arguments for wanting to make exclusive decisions to enable them to cope with and manage sometimes worrying and disturbing behaviour. Equally, where children's difficulties are located in the context of parental discord, abuse, domestic violence or family dynamics it is important to ensure children are not blamed or scapegoated for problems caused by events or actions outside their control (Cooper et al., 1999; Sutton, 1999; Dallos and Draper, 2000).

Research evidence demonstrates the value of consulting children and seeing how much they can achieve with a little help which is appropriate and acceptable. Children, like adults, have the right, under the terms of the UN Convention, to be consulted with, and to express their views about, services provided for them (UN, 1989, Article 12). In public services in England and Wales there is a legal duty to consult children in order to ascertain their wishes and feelings (Children Act, 1989).

In seeking to ascertain the perceptions of children and young people about mental health services the primary ethical consideration is to prevent any harm or wrongdoing during the process of evaluation. While respecting children's competencies you need to also fulfil your responsibilities to protect children and young people. The following issues need to be considered:

- There is considerable uncertainty about the issue of children's consent to participate in evaluative research. The issue has yet to be fully tested in court.

- Researchers need to consider actively involving children to select topics, plan research or advise on monitoring research.

- The timing of evaluation with children and young people with mental health problems, feedback to them, and the dissemination of findings, require careful and sensitive consideration.

The language of children's needs permeates the professional literature, policy guidance and legislative frameworks that contextualise modern practice with children and young people. Replacing the concept of children's needs with that of children's rights offers a direct challenge to the paternalistic protectionist constructions that emphasise children as powerless dependents who are effectively excluded from participating in shaping their own environment. The idea that such provision is in the best interests of the child is a commonly used justification but quite meaningless. In child and adolescent mental health this means adopting a child's eye view of the world and enlisting them in designing more relevant needs assessment models and accessible support services. Interests like needs are not a quality of the child but a matter of cultural interpretation that is context-specific and open to multiple interpretations (Woodhead, 1997).

Activity 6.3

a) Think back to when you were about 14 years of age and how often you were asked for your opinion. Did you feel listened to?

b) Now consider your own children or service users of about the same age and note down the differences in the amount and quality of consultation that is offered.

Effective planning and management

Evaluation involves the collection, analysis and interpretation of data bearing on your or your agency's goals and programme objectives. Evaluation usually attempts to measure the extent to which certain outcomes can be correlated with inputs. These quantifiable indicators of performance can provide evidence of the extent to which specified targets are being met. The culture of evaluation in public services has become prominent in the 1980s and 1990s as social and economic changes have introduced privatised services, welfare cutbacks, and a mixed economy of care in which recipients of services are defined as consumers.

In attempting to match resources and services to service users expectations and perceived needs, you are faced with increasing and more complex demands to improve efficiency and effectiveness. Central to all this is the concept of quality assurance which demands a commitment to the pursuit of a high standard of services. Policy statements setting out performance indicators in all areas of health and social care practice stress the essential role of monitoring and evaluation. It is useful to think about evaluation and distinguish between subjective and objective approaches. Subjective evaluation concentrates on gauging how children and young people have experienced what you and your agency have offered them. Objective evaluation involves identifying particular objectives in the work and then deciding whether or not these have been achieved.

Subjective evaluation could be carried out either through discussion or through some form of questionnaire. Or you might also wish to think about how, in devising a questionnaire, you could focus on partnership and empowerment by:

- Asking specific questions on degree of involvement, for example whether the child felt they were properly listened to.

- Working together with the service user to make sure the questionnaire reflected their agenda.

- Looking at whether the outcome of intervention was satisfactory, and if not how it could be done differently.

- Tackling issues of power and discrimination such as asking particular questions related to the service user's needs as a black child, refugee, woman, or someone with a disability.

Objective evaluation could mean your objectives will depend on your particular work setting. The important point is that they are clearly measurable, for example:

- Removal from the child protection register, or return home.

- A young person finding accommodation or a job.

- Reducing the risk of suicide or self-harming behaviour.

- Finding an adoptive family.

- Improving a child's school attendance.

- Reducing incidents of aggressive behaviour.

Activity 6.4

a) Imagine that your agency has been criticised for the way it evaluates its services. You are about to make a brief presentation of your initial thoughts on how evaluation in CAMHS might be improved.

b) Think about how you might use subjective and objective evaluation in your work.

Many practitioners tend to avoid evaluation or to interpret it in such a way that it comes to mean a brief retrospective review of a piece of work or an initiative. You may also hold the view that your agency has to collect so much performance-related information for the government that anything that appears to detract from work with service users and your primary responsibilities has to be avoided. However accountable practice demands that public services need to justify what they do and find useful ways of demonstrating this.

An action evaluation model has been developed in Bradford (Fawcett, 2000) which is based on a partnership between the university, social services department, and the health trust aimed at demystifying the evaluation process and providing staff with the tools and support to conduct evaluations. Action evaluations take place in the workplace, and focus on areas viewed as important by those involved, with the findings feeding into the services being studied. These are the main characteristics:

- **Outline the current situation** – collect baseline information and establish the service's overall aims and objectives. This can include quantitative data such as the numbers using a service, and qualitative data such as details of service users' experiences.

- **Specify available resources, overall aim and objectives** – any project or initiative is likely to have a number of objectives but it is important to be specific about them and what the broad overall purpose of the activity is.

- **Link goals to specific objectives** – identifying the desired outcomes or goals enable you to work backwards through any intermediary stages in the process. This helps to provide progress indicators and how goals can be achieved.

- **Detail why the agreed objectives and goals were decided upon** – no evaluation goes strictly according to plan therefore it is important to record how goals were established. A record needs to be kept of the reasoning behind the aims, and any deviation clearly stated and made transparent. This information needs to be easily retrievable so it can be used to explain why goals have changed.

- **Monitor and review the activity** – information from all the stakeholders can be collated including recommendations for changing or improving the service. Activity related to goals can be appraised, and evidence of progress summarised. It is important to document how and why progress was made and what obstacles were encountered. This data can be fed back to service purchasers and planners reflecting an inclusive, bottom-up approach to evaluation.

■ LEARNING REVIEW

In this chapter we have explained why practice should be evidence based and also how it is linked to the change process. The concept of change has been examined in the context of the lack of a substantive evidence base in what is effective intervention in CAMHS.

We have identified methods of practice evaluation that are synonymous with service user participation. The perceptions of children and young people are largely absent from the current data on evaluating CAMHS making this an important area for future research at the practitioner level. The importance of involving clients in evaluation using a children's rights perspective with ethical considerations has been highlighted.

We have discussed how evaluation can contribute to the effective planning and management of CAMHS at both practice and agency levels as a means of contributing to the growing evidence base. This will enable practitioners to measure their own personal effectiveness and help further improve quality standards in CAMHS provision.

References and further reading

Alderson P (2000) *Young Children's Rights*. London, Save the Children/Jessica Kingsley.

Audit Commission (1999) *Children in Mind: Child and Adolescent Mental Health Services*. London, HMSO.

Barlow J (1998) Parent Training Programmes and Behaviour Problems: Findings From a Systematic Review. In Buchanan A and Hudson B (Eds.) *Parenting, Schooling, and Children's Behaviour: Interdisciplinary Approaches*. Alton, Ashgate.

Barnes, McGuire J, Stein A and Rosenberg W (1997) Evidence Based Medicine and Child Mental Health Services. A Broad Approach to Evaluation is Needed. *Children and Society*. 11: 89-96.

Barton J (1999) Child and Adolescent Psychiatry. In Hill M (Ed.) *Effective Ways Of Working With Children and Their Families*. London, Jessica Kingsley.

Bernzweig J et al. (1997) Gender Differences in Physician-Patient Communication. *Archives of Paediatric Adolescent Medicine*. 151: 586-91.

Carr A (Ed.) (2000). *What Works for Children and Adolescents? A Critical Review of Psychological Interventions With Children, Adolescents and Their Families*. London, Routledge.

Cederborg A (1997) Young Children's Participation in Family Therapy Talk. *The American Journal of Family Therapy*. 25: 28-38.

Child Psychotherapy Trust (1998) *Is Child Psychotherapy Effective?* London, CPT.

Cooper P (Ed.) (1999) *Understanding and Supporting Children with Emotional and Behavioural Difficulties*. London, Jessica Kingsley.

Dallos R and Draper R (2000) *An Introduction to Family Therapy*. Buckingham, OU Press.

Fawcett B (2000) *Look, listen and learn*. Community Care. July.

Finch J (1987) The Vignette Technique in Survey Research. *Sociology.* 21: 1, 105-14.

Gordon G and Grant R (1997) *How we Feel: An Insight Into the Emotional World of Teenagers.* London, Jessica Kingsley.

Gowers S et al. (1999) Brief Scale for Measuring the Outcomes of Emotional and Behavioural Disorders in Children. *British Journal of Psychiatry.* 174: 413-6.

Gowers S et al. (2000) The Health of the Nation Outcome Scales for Child and Adolescent Mental Health. *Child Psychology and Psychiatry Review.* 5: 2, 50-6.

Graham P (1996) The Thirty Year Contribution of Research into Child Mental Health to Clinical Practice and Public Policy in the UK. In Bernstein B and Brannen J (Eds.) *Children Research and Policy.* London, Taylor and Francis.

Greenbaum T (1987) *The Practical Handbook and Guide to Focus Group Research.* Lexington, Lexington Books.

Hazel N (1995) *Seen and Heard: An Examination of Methods for Collecting Data From Young People.* Guildford, University of Surrey.

Hennessey E (1999) Children as Service Evaluators. *Child Psychology and Psychiatry Review.* 4: 4, 153-61.

Hill M (1999) *Effective Ways of Working With Children and Their Families.* London, Jessica Kingsley.

Hill M, Laybourn A and Borland M (1996) Engaging with Primary-Age Children About Their Emotions and Well-Being: Methodological Considerations. *Children and Society.* 10: 129-44.

Hunter J, Higginson I and Garralda E (1996) Systematic Literature Review: Outcome Measures for Child and Adolescent Mental Health Services. *Journal of Public Health Medicine.* 18: 197-206.

Kent H and Read J (1998) Measuring Consumer Participation in Mental Health Services: Are Attitudes Related to Professional Orientation? *International Journal of Social Psychiatry.* 44: 4, 295-310.

Laws S et al. (1999). *Time to Listen: Young People's Experiences of Mental Health Services.* London, Save the Children.

McNeish D, Newman T and Roberts H (2002) *What Works? Effective Social Care Services for Children and Families.* Buckingham, OU Press.

MacFarlane A and McPherson A (1995) Primary Healthcare and Adolescence. *British Medical Journal.* 311: 825-6.

Marshal M, Feldman R and Sigal J (1989) The Unravelling of a Treatment Paradigm: A Follow-Up Study of the Milan Approach to Family Therapy. *Family Process*. 28: 457-70.

Mas C, Alexander J and Barton C (1985) Modes of Expression in Family Therapy: A Process Study of Roles and Gender. *Journal of Family and Marital Therapy*. 11: 411-5.

May T (Ed.) (2002) *Qualitative Research in Action*. London, Sage.

Mental Health Foundation (1999) *The Big Picture: Promoting Children and Young People's Mental Health*. London, Mental Health Foundation.

Pollard A (1987) Studying Childrens Perspectives: A Collaborative Approach. In Walford G (Ed.) *Doing Sociology of Education*. Lewes, Falmer Press.

Polowczyk D (1993) Comparison of Patient and Staff Surveys of Consumer Satisfaction. *Hospital and Community Psychiatry*. 14: 4, 88-95.

Richardson J and Joughin C (2000) *The Mental Health Needs of Looked After Children*. London, Gaskell.

Rogers C (1957) The Necessary and Sufficient Conditions of Therapeutic Personality Change. *Journal of Consulting Psychology*. 21: 95-103.

Sanford M et al. (1992) Ontario Child Health Study: Social and School Impairments in Children Aged 6-16 Years. *Journal of the American Academy of Child and Adolescent Psychiatry*. 31: 1, 66-75.

Shaw I (1996) *Evaluating in Practice*. Aldershot, Arena.

Sheldon B and Chilvers R (2000) *Evidence-based Social Care*. Lyme Regis, Russell House.

Smith S et al. (1996) The Voices of Children: Pre Adolescent Children's Experiences in Family Therapy. *Journal of Marital and Family Therapy*. 22: 69-86.

Strickland Clark L, Campbell D and Dallos R (2000) Children's and Adolescent's Views on Family Therapy. *Journal of Family Therapy*. 22: 324-41.

Sutton C (1999) *Helping Families with Troubled Children*. London, Wiley.

Target M and Fonagy P (1996) The Psychological Treatment of Child and Adolescent Psychiatric Disorders. In Roth A and Fonagy P (Eds.) *What Works for Whom? A Critical Review of Psychotherapy Research*. New York, The Guilford Press.

Treseder P (1997) *Empowering Children and Young People: A Training Manual for Promoting Involvement in Decision-Making*. London, Save the Children.

Triseliotis J (1995) *Teenagers and the Social Work Services.* London, HMSO.

Vasta R, Haith R and Miller S (1993) *Child Psychology.* John Wiley, New York.

Walker S (2001) Consulting with Children and Young People. *The International Journal of Children's Rights.* 9: 45-56.

Wilson J (1999) *Child Focused Practice.* London, Karnac Books.

Woodhead M (1997) Psychology and the Cultural Construction of Children's Needs. In James A and Prout A (Eds.) *Constructing and Reconstructing Childhood.* London, Falmer Press.

Conclusion and learning review

The greatest chance of positive change in children with conduct problems and emotional difficulties consistent with early signs of mental health problems lies mainly in improvements in their family circumstances, positive peer group relationships, and good school experiences, and less in direct contact with specialist child psychiatric services'.

(Rutter, 1991)

This statement from a leading child and adolescent psychiatrist is testimony to the notion that a great deal of important and helpful work can be undertaken in the area of child and adolescent mental health by all staff in contact with children and young people. This means you do not necessarily have to be a child psychiatrist to help the majority of children and young people who are troubled. Building on some basic skills in social care, nursing, youth work or teaching you can make a valuable contribution to the process of assessment and intervention in the lives of children. The evidence demonstrates that a little help can go a long way especially if that involves enabling other staff, parents or young people themselves to realise that the child's difficulties are connected to mental health issues that are relatively common and treatable.

We have examined and reviewed a number of key practical and theoretical resources for practitioners in a variety of contexts in voluntary or statutory agencies who may encounter situations where concerns are expressed about the behaviour, emotional state, or mental health of a child or young person. If your work involves nursing, social work or teaching in the context of child protection, primary care, young offenders, family support, long-term planning, paediatric nursing, fostering and adoption, youth work, juvenile justice, education and probation then this workbook has hopefully helped develop your practice. The foundational ideas and practical guidance have been designed to support you in an accessible and sometimes challenging format to create the basis for informed, reflective, confident practice.

This may provide the foundation for you to build a more progressive and advanced knowledge and skills base to continue to improve your practice and expertise in particular areas such as counselling, psychotherapy, or family therapy for example. The workbook may also have filled a gap in your learning or reinforced and reaffirmed your practice knowledge and skills to enable you to continue in your work with renewed confidence and energy. If this workbook has met your needs then it will have served its purpose or if it has not and requires changes then I would value your feedback and comments in due course. The important thing in a text like this is that it has stimulated your thinking and reflection about the subject and if only in a small way has made a difference to your practice. Because that difference may make all the difference to the child or young person you are working with.

Use the following checklist to review your learning having studied this workbook. Compare it with your Learning Profile completed before you began. If there are any areas where it seems your knowledge has not developed sufficiently, revisit the chapters in question, and then, if necessary, compare your progress with a colleague, or supervisor. Select some of the suggested further reading in those areas requiring attention. You may in any case want to consider training or further professional development opportunities to continue to develop your practice in this area. A list of selected resources and organisations directly or indirectly connected to child and adolescent mental health practice or research is included at the end of the workbook.

Chapter 1: Multi-disciplinary working

	Not at all	Partly	Very well
I can:			
Explain the importance of multi-disciplinary working	❏	❏	❏
Describe the obstacles to, and ways to achieve effective multi-disciplinary work	❏	❏	❏
Describe how changing patterns of service delivery are influencing professional relationships	❏	❏	❏
Work in partnership to identify and analyse potential problems and appropriate responses	❏	❏	❏

Chapter 2: Definitions, prevalence and assessment

	Not at all	Partly	Very well
I can:			
Describe the differences between mental health, mental health problem, and mental disorder	❏	❏	❏
Explain the importance of theories of human growth and development	❏	❏	❏
Describe risk and resilience factors in children and young people	❏	❏	❏
Explain how knowledge, skills and values are integrated in effective assessment	❏	❏	❏

Chapter 3: Culturally competent practice

	Not at all	Partly	Very well

I can:

	Not at all	Partly	Very well
Describe what is meant by culturally competent practice	❑	❑	❑
Illustrate the importance of cultural identity to the mental health of a diverse society	❑	❑	❑
Explain how understanding of oppression and discrimination influences contemporary practice	❑	❑	❑
Describe the mental health needs of black and ethnic minority families	❑	❑	❑

Chapter 4: The organisational and legal context

I can:

	Not at all	Partly	Very well
Describe the four tier model of CAMHS organisation	❑	❑	❑
Describe the main legislative framework for CAMHS	❑	❑	❑
Explain how CAMHS fits with other children's services	❑	❑	❑
Identify how different agencies conceptualise children and young people's mental health problems	❑	❑	❑

Chapter 5: Planning and intervention

	Not at all	Partly	Very well
I can:			
Integrate knowledge, skills and values in analysing information and weighing its significance and priority	❏	❏	❏
Demonstrate how an assessment leads to a set of concrete objectives for intervention	❏	❏	❏
Describe the importance of reflective practice and supervision	❏	❏	❏
Identify in partnership with clients the appropriate model and method of intervention that best meets their needs	❏	❏	❏

Chapter 6: Effectiveness and evaluation

	Not at all	Partly	Very well
I can:			
Explain why practice should be evidence based	❏	❏	❏
Identify methods of practice evaluation	❏	❏	❏
Involve clients in evaluation using a children's rights perspective	❏	❏	❏
Explain how evaluation can contribute to the effective planning and management of CAMHS at both practice and agency levels	❏	❏	❏

Advisory Centre for Education
1b Aberdeen Studios
22-24 Highbury Grove
London N5 2EA
Tel: 020 7354 8321

Asian Family Counselling Services
74 The Avenue
London W13 8LB
Tel: 020 8997 5749

Asylum Aid
244a Upper Street
London N1 1RU
Tel: 020 7359 4026
www.asylumaid.org.uk

Barnardos
Tanners Lane
Barkingside
Essex IG6 1QG
Tel: 020 8550 8822
www.barnardos.ie

Black Information Link
The 1990 Trust
9 Cranmer Road
London SW9 6EJ
Tel: 020 7582 1990
www.blink.org.uk

Child Poverty Action Group
1-5 Bath Street
London EC1V 9PY
Tel: 020 7253 3406

Child Psychotherapy Trust
Star House
104-108 Grafton Road
London NW5 4BD
Tel: 020 7284 1355
www.cpt.co.uk

Childline
2nd Floor, Royal Mail Building
50 Studd Street
London N1 0QW
Tel: 020 7239 1000
www.childline.org.uk

Children's Legal Centre
University of Essex
Wivenhoe Park
Colchester
Essex CO4 3SQ
Tel: 01206 873820
www.essex.ac.uk/clc

Children's Rights Office
City Road
London EC1V 1LJ
Tel: 020 7278 8222
www.cro.org.uk

Children's Society
Edward Rudolf House
Margery Street
London WC1X 0JL
Tel: 020 7841 4436
www.the-childrens-society.org.uk

Commission for Racial Equality
Elliot House
10-12 Allington Street
London SW1E 5EH
Tel: 020 7828 7022
www.cre.gov.uk

Coram Family
Coram Community Campus
49 Mecklenburgh Square
London WC1N 2QA
Tel: 020 7520 0300
www.coram.org.uk

Disability Now
6 Market Road
London N7 9PW
Tel: 020 7619 7323
www.disabilitynow.org.uk

Drugscope
32-36 Longman Street
London SE1 0EE
Tel: 020 7928 1771
www.drugscope.org.uk

FOCUS
The Royal College of Psychiatrists
College Research Unit
6th Floor
83 Victoria Street
London SW1H 0HW
Tel: 020 7227 0821
www.rcpsych.ac.uk/cru

Families Need Fathers
134 Curtain Road
London EC2A 3AR
Tel: 020 7613 5060
www.fnf.org.uk

Family Rights Group
The Print House
18 Ashwin Street
London E8 3DL
Tel: 020 7923 2628
www.frg.co.uk

Home Start
2 Salisbury Road
Leicester LE1 7QR
Tel: 011 6233 9955
www.home-start.org.uk

Institute of Family Therapy
24-32 Stephenson Way
London NW1 2HV
Tel: 020 7391 9150
www.ift.org.uk

Kidscape
2 Grosvenor Gardens
London SW1W 9TR
Tel: 020 7730 3300
www.kidscape.org.uk

MIND
Granta House
15-19 Broadway
London E15 4BQ
Tel: 020 8522 1728
www.mind.org.uk

Mental Health Foundation
20-21 Cornwall Terrace
London NW1 4QL
Tel: 020 7535 7400
www.mentalhealth.org.uk

NCH Action for Children
85 Highbury Park
London N5 1UD
Tel: 020 7704 7000
www.nchafc.org.uk

NSPCC
National Centre
42 Curtain Road
London EC2A 3NH
Tel: 020 7825 2500
www.nspcc.org.uk

FSIYAT
Intercultural Therapy Centre
278 Seven Sisters Road,
London N4 2HY
Tel: 020 7263 4130

**National Association of Young
People's Counselling and Advisory
Services**
17-23 Albion Road
Leicester LE1 6GD
Tel: 01642 816846

National Autistic Society
393 City Road
London EC1V 1NE
Tel: 020 7833 2299

National Centre for Eating Disorders
54 New Road
Esher KT10 9NU
Tel: 01372 469493
www.eating-disorders.org.uk

National Children's Bureau
8 Wakley Street
London EC1V 7QE
Tel: 020 7843 6000
www.ncb.org.uk

**National Family and Parenting
Institute**
520 Highgate Studios
53-79 Highgate Road
London NW5 1TL
Tel: 020 7424 3460
www.nfpi.org.uk

National Pyramid Trust
204 Church Road
London W7 3BP
Tel: 020 8579 5108

Parentline Plus
520 Highgate Studios
53-79 Highgate Road
London NW5 1TL
Tel: 020 7209 2460
www.parentlineplus.org.uk

Race Equality Unit
27/28 Angel Gate
City Road
London EC1V 2PT
Tel: 020 7278 2331
www.reunet.demon.co.uk

Refugee Council
Bondway House
3-9 Bondway
London SW8 1SJ
Tel: 020 7820 3000

Save the Children
17 Grove Lane
London SE5 8RD
Tel: 020 7703 5400
www.savethechildren.org.uk

Stepfamilies UK
www.stepfamilies.co.uk

Tavistock Institute
120 Belsize Lane
London NW3 5BA
Tel: 0207 435 7111
www.tav-port.org.uk

Trust for the Study of Adolescence
23 New Road
Brighton BN1 1WZ
Tel: 01273 693311
www.tsa.uk.com

Values into Action
Oxford House, Derbyshire Street
London E2 6HG
Tel: 020 7729 5436

Voice for the Child in Care
Unit 4 Pride Court
80-82 White Lion Street
London N1 9PF
Tel: 020 7833 5792

Who Cares Trust
Kemp House
152-160 City Road
London EC1V 2NP
Tel: 020 7251 3117
www.thewhocarestrust.org.uk

Women's Aid Federation
PO Box 391
Bristol BS99 7WS
Tel: 08457 023468

YMCA Dads and Lads Project
Dee Bridge House
25-27 Lower Bridge Street
Chester CH1 1RS
Tel: 01244 403090

Young Minds
The National Association for Child
and Family Mental Health
102-108 Clerkenwell Road
London EC1M 5SA
Tel: 020 7336 8445
www.youngminds.org.uk

Youth Access
2 Taylors Yard
67 Alderbrook Road
London SW12 8AD
Tel: 020 8772 9900
www.yacess.co.uk

Youth in Mind
www.youthinmind.net

Photocopiable activities and tables

Activity 1.1

a) Select a child or young person from your caseload. Write their name in the centre of a large piece of paper and then draw around them the professionals and other helping staff involved at some time in their care.

b) Now examine the staff involved and make a list of those who you feel close to and those who you do not. Explain the differences.

Activity 1.2

a) Obtain a copy of your local CAMHS strategy document.

b) Discuss this with your line manager or supervisor and clarify your role in relation to it and your agency's responsibilities.

Activity 1.3

a) In partnership with a colleague from another agency select a closed case you were both previously engaged with.

b) Review and reflect on the process of multi-disciplinary working, highlighting where things went wrong, where things went well, and why.

Activity 1.4

a) Make contact with a different practitioner from another agency involved in your local CAMHS.

b) Together, draw up an action plan of how to improve inter-agency communication and review this in 3 months.

Activity 2.1

a) Consult with your friends, neighbours, relatives and partner about their perceptions of the behaviour and emotional world of children and young people these days.

b) Now consider these impressions with the data on prevalence and causation and explain the differences.

Activity 2.2

a) Review the information above on developmental theories and select the one or those that fit with your beliefs about the influences on people.

b) Now use it/them to construct your own personal developmental process and make an assessment of yourself at age 13.

Activity 2.3

a) Using details of a child or young person from your caseload write a list of three risk factors and three resilience factors.

b) Now weigh them up and decide whether the balance falls towards risk or resilience.

Activity 2.4

a) Together with a colleague, each write down three lists of your own characteristics at age 7 as you felt, as your parents saw you, and as your class teacher perceived you.

b) Note the similarities and differences, and think about and discuss together what concepts informed those differences.

Activity 3.1

a) Buy a selection of weekend newspapers and spend some time looking through them to see whether and how cultural diversity is represented.

b) Now consider the area or population your agency serves and ask yourself whether it is accessible to every member of the community.

Activity 3.2

a) Together with a colleague find a copy of your agency's equal opportunities policy and discuss the implications for your own personal practice.

b) Each argues the case for and against a black member of staff being allocated to a black or other ethnic minority family.

Activity 3.3

a) Write down a list of the ethnic minority groups in your community and against each one write a stereotypical characteristic relating to their personalities.

b) Now imagine two teenage girls, one white Irish, the other Pakistani, described as quiet, withdrawn and depressed. Think about the reasons for differences and similarities in your assessment and intervention plan.

Activity 3.4

a) Pick three specific elements of culturally competent practice that are the most important to you.

b) Now make an action plan to put into practice those three elements and review your progress in three months time.

Activity 4.1

a) Examine Table 4.2 and find out where your agency is placed in the CAMHS structure.

b) Find out from your line manager or agency guidelines what the protocols are for referring children and adolescents between the four-tier CAMHS structure.

Activity 4.2

a) Together with a colleague review the above material relating to the legal context of CAMHS. Each of you draws up a list of the three most important points. Discuss and compare your answers.

b) Think about a child or young person you have recently helped and draw a diagram showing the number of agencies involved with them and their legal context.

Activity 4.3

a) Think about a time in your childhood when you felt worried or very upset about something but were unable to talk to anyone about it. Looking back, what would you liked to have happened or what would you have liked a trusted adult to say to you which would have enabled you to talk?

b) Find a copy of your employer's policy on client confidentiality or talk to your line manager about the issue and any guidelines that are available. Discuss who to contact when dilemmas about confidentiality occur.

Activity 4.4

a) Select a child or young person you have worked with and write down the main reasons for the referral to your agency and the initial assessment. Now imagine you worked in two different agencies with the same client and write down the assessment from their two different agency perspectives.

b) Now write one referral and one assessment using the language of the child or young person as they would describe their problems.

Activity 5.1

a) You have assessed a young person aged 14 years with a history of drug abuse and depressive illness. There is also a history of parental disharmony and domestic violence. Make a list of the advantages and disadvantages of family therapy.

b) Now put yourself in the place of the young person and see what options appeal most to you.

Activity 5.2

a) A pattern of referrals has been noticed in recent months during the warmer weather of children and young people congregating in well-known meeting places for disaffected youth abusing drugs. There are some background issues suggestive of emerging mental health problems. Make a list of the potential stakeholders required to intervene in this situation.

b) How are you going to convince these young people and the other stakeholders of the benefits of participating in any response to this situation?

Activity 5.3

a) You have been working individually with a female child aged 9 for three months on a weekly basis, following a period of school refusal/phobia. The child is now happier, less anxious and sociable but adamant she is not returning to school. The multi-agency professionals involved are split on how to proceed.

b) How do you make sense of this situation and what theoretical and practical resources can help you?

Activity 5.4

a) Spend ten minutes thinking about the constraints on planning intervention in child and adolescent mental health work.

b) Discuss your findings with a colleague or supervisor and consider the strategies you might use for managing.

Activity 6.1

a) Together with a colleague discuss your agency's policy and procedures for evaluating practice.

b) How does this information inform the practice of individual practitioners?

Activity 6.2

a) Spend a little time reflecting on a recent period of work and the way cases were assessed for effectiveness.

b) Now consider how the reviews/summaries/conclusions could be collated to inform future practice changes.

Activity 6.3

a) Think back to when you were about 14 years of age and how often
    you were asked for your opinion. Did you feel listened to?

b) Now consider your own children or service users of about the same
    age and note down the differences in the amount and quality of
    consultation that is offered.

Activity 6.4

a) Imagine that your agency has been criticised for the way it evaluates
    its services. You are about to make a brief presentation of your initial
    thoughts on how evaluation in CAMHS might be improved.

b) Think about how you might use subjective and objective evaluation
    in your work.

Learning outcomes

1. Contribute to the understanding and assessment of the mental health needs and problems of children, adolescents and young people.

2. Communicate and engage with young people in a process of partnership practice that enables them to identify and articulate their needs and agendas.

3. Demonstrate critical understanding of current policy and legal aspects of working with children, young people, and their families.

4. Demonstrate knowledge and awareness of the importance of culturally competent practice.

5. Communicate effectively in partnership with multi-disciplinary staff in delivering the care needs of children, adolescents and their families.

6. Contribute to the effective planning and use of methods and models of intervention with clients.

7. Demonstrate knowledge of the requirements for evidence-based practice and the importance of effective evaluation.

Table 1.1: Areas for consideration when planning multi-disciplinary care

Initial discussion	Identify core group staff	Collate contributions to plan	Specify meeting dates	Clarify responsibility boundaries	Clarify assessment depth
The core group	Purpose and function	Methods to promote participatory practice	Anticipate potential inter-agency problems	Agree protocols for more attendees	Management of meeting-minutes, feedback
The plan	Overall aim	Timescale to implement	Methods to engage child and family	Agree procedures for changes to plan	Evaluation and plan monitoring
The key worker	Co-ordination	Direct work with child or family	Keeping an overview	Clarify joint working tasks	Manage inter-agency problems
The review	The remit of the review	Delegation of core group decisions	Guidance on reporting to the review	Enabling contributions from child and family	Providing support to staff

After Horwath and Calder, 1998.

Table 2.1: Prevalence of specific child and adolescent mental health problems

Emotional disorders	4.5-9.9% of 10 year olds
Major depression	0.5-2.5% of children, 2-8% of adolescents
Conduct disorders	6.2-10.8% of 10 year olds
Tic disorders	1-13% of boys, 1-11% of girls
Obsessive compulsive disorder	1.9% of adolescents
Hyperkinetic disorder (ADHD)	1 in 200 of all children
Encopresis (faecal soiling)	2.3% of boys, 0.7% of girls aged 7-8 years
Anorexia nervosa	0.5%-1% of 12-19 year olds
Bulimia nervosa	1% of adolescent girls and young women
Attempted suicide	2-4% of adolescents
Suicide	7.6 per 100,000 15-19 year olds
Alcohol abuse	29% of all 13 year olds drink weekly
Cannabis	3-5% of 11-16 year olds have used
Heroin and cocaine	Less than 1%
Hallucinogens	Increase reported

DoH, 1995

Table 2.2: Factors that are known to increase the risk of mental health problems in children and young people

- **Child risk factors:**
  - genetic influences
  - low IQ and learning disability
  - specific developmental delay
  - communication difficulty
  - difficult temperament
  - physical illness, especially if chronic and/or neurological
  - academic failure
  - low self-esteem

- **Family risk situations:**
  - overt parental conflict
  - family breakdown
  - inconsistent or unclear discipline
  - hostile and rejecting relationships
  - failure to adapt to a child's changing developmental needs
  - abuse – physical, sexual or emotional
  - parental psychiatric illness
  - parental criminality, alcoholism, and personality disorder
  - death and loss – including loss of friendships

- **Environmental risk factors:**
  - socio-economic disadvantage
  - homelessness
  - disaster
  - discrimination
  - other significant life events

Audit Commission, 1998.

Table 3.1: People born outside Great Britain and resident here, by countries of birth, 1991

Countries of birth	No. resident in Britain	% of Britain's population
Northern Ireland	245,000	0.45
Irish Republic	592,000	1.08
Germany	216,000	0.39
Italy	91,000	0.17
France	53,000	0.10
Other EC	133,900	0.24
Scandinavia and EFTA	58,300	0.11
E. Europe and former USSR	142,900	0.26
Cyprus	78,000	0.14
Rest of Near and Middle East	58,300	0.11
Aust, NZ and Canada	177,400	0.32
New Commonwealth	1,688,400	3.08
Jamaica	142,000	0.26
Rest of Caribbean	122,600	0.22
India	409,000	0.75
Pakistan	234,000	0.43
Bangladesh	105,000	0.19
Rest of South Asia	39,500	0.07
South East Asia	150,400	0.27
East Africa	220,600	0.40
West and Southern Africa	110,700	0.20
Rest of the World	566,200	1.03
Asia	231,000	0.42
North Africa	44,600	0.08
South Africa	68,000	0.12
Rest of Africa	34,300	0.06
USA	143,000	0.26
Rest of Americas	42,000	0.08
Total born outside GB	**3,991,000**	**7.27**

Owen, 1992-1995.

Table 4.1: CAMHS service provider guidelines

Relationships with commissioners

- The service should be represented on a group that regularly advises commissioners and purchasers about arrangements for delivering comprehensive child and adolescent mental health services.
- The CAMHS should have a plan which reflects an understanding of how the purchaser perceives the contribution of this specialist service as part of the delivery of the full child and adolescent mental health service.

Top level trust planning

- There should be an operational policy for CAMHS.
- There should be a recognisable and separate budget for the CAMHS.
- There should be an awareness of the major elements of CAMHS expenditure.
- Services should be child-centred and responsive to age-related and other particular needs, such as those of families from minority ethnic groups.
- Services should have protocols for dealing with confidentiality.
- Services should be provided in a welcoming environment, with buildings and rooms safe and suitable for children and young people.
- There should be service level agreements to cover consultancy and advice for consultant colleagues in other specialties such as paediatrics. Agreements should ensure that the service provides regular and adequate input to children's homes, EBD schools, secure units, and to other groups of young people at particular risk.
- There should be provision for adequate specialist mental health support to social workers, teachers, GPs and others.
- The CAMHS should be provided by a multi-disciplinary team or through a network. Health service personnel will make up only a part of the team – appropriate input from social services and education departments should also be maintained.
- There should be a clear relationship with adult mental health services.

Operations

- There should be an adequate information system geared specifically to CAMHS.
- The service should offer a relevant range of interventions to suit different needs.
- There should be clear referral channels to CAMHS which are appropriate to the referrer.
- There should be a clear access route to day patient and in-patient services.
- There should be a clear protocol for dealing with young people who present in crisis – including those who may deliberately harm themselves. There should be access to adequate and appropriately skilled 24 hour cover by mental health specialists for the child and adolescent population.
- Waiting time for the first appointment for a non-urgent condition should be less than 13 weeks.
- The service should identify topics for audit which should be undertaken regularly.
- Appropriate training should be offered to CAMHS staff, including secretarial and reception staff.

Audit Commission, 1998.

Table 4.2: CAMHS tiered framework

Key components, professionals and functions of tiered child and adolescent mental health services	
Tier 1. A primary level which includes interventions by: • GPs • health visitors • school nurses • social services • voluntary agencies • teachers • residential social workers • juvenile justice workers Child and adolescent mental health services (CAMHS) at this level are provided by non-specialists who are in a position to: • Identify mental health problems early in their development. • Offer general advice – and in certain cases treatment for less severe problems. • Pursue opportunities for promoting mental health and preventing mental health problems.	**Tier 3. A specialist service for the more severe, complex and persistent disorders. This is usually a multi-disciplinary team or service working in a community child mental health clinic or child psychiatry out-patient service, and including:** • child and adolescent psychiatrists • social workers • clinical psychologists • community psychiatric nurses • child psychotherapists • occupational therapists • art, music and drama therapists The core CAMHS in each district should be able to offer: • Assessment and treatment of child mental health disorders. • Assessment for referrals to Tier 4. • Contribution to the services, consultation and training at Tiers 1 and 2. • Participation in R and D projects.
Tier 2. A level of service provided by uni-professional group which relates to others through a network (rather than within a team). These include: • clinical child psychologists • paediatricians, especially community • educational psychologists • child psychiatrists • community child psychiatric nurses • nurse specialists CAMHS professionals should be able to offer: • Training and consultation to other professionals (who might be within Tier 1). • Consultation for professionals and families. • Outreach to identify severe or complex needs which require more specialist interventions but where the children or families are unwilling to use specialist services. • Assessment which may trigger treatment at a different tier.	**Tier 4. Access to infrequently used but essential tertiary level services such as day units, highly specialist out-patient teams, and in-patient units for older children and adolescents who are severely mentally ill or at suicidal risk. These services may need to be provided on a supra-district level as not all districts can expect to offer this level of expertise.** The most specialist CAMHS may provide for more than one district or region, and should be able to offer a range of services which might include: • adolescent in-patient units • secure forensic adolescent units • eating disorder units • specialist teams for sexual abuse • specialist teams for neuro-psychiatric problems

Based on *A Handbook on Child and Adolescent Mental Health*, DoH and DoE, 1995.

Table 4.3: Agency responses to the same presenting problem

Juvenile justice	Social services	Education	Psychiatry
Aggression	Aggression	Aggression	Aggression
Referral to police: decision to charge ↓	Referral to social services ↓	Referral to education department ↓	Referral to child psychiatrist ↓
Pre-sentence report completed ↓	Social work assessment conducted ↓	Educational psychology assessment ↓	Psychiatric assessment ↓
Sentenced to custody ↓	Decision to accommodate ↓	Placed in residential school ↓	Admitted to regional in-patient unit ↓
Labelled as young offender	Labelled as beyond parental control	Labelled as having learning difficulty	Labelled as mentally ill

After Malek, 1993.

Table 5.1: Strengths and difficulties questionnaire

	Not true	Somewhat true	Certainly true
Considerate of other peoples feelings			
Restless, overactive, cannot stay still for long			
Often complains of headaches, stomach-aches			
Shares readily with other children			
Often has temper tantrums or hot tempers			
Rather solitary, tends to play alone			
Generally obedient, usually does what adults ask			
Many worries, often seems worried			
Helpful if someone is hurt, upset or feeling ill			
Has at least one good friend			
Constantly fidgeting or squirming			
Often fights with other children or bullies them			
Often unhappy, down-hearted or tearful			
Generally liked by other children			
Easily distracted, concentration wanders			
Nervous or clingy in new situations, easily loses confidence			
Kind to younger children			
Often lies or cheats			
Picked on or bullied by other children			
Often volunteers to help others			
Thinks things out before acting			
Steals from home, school or elsewhere			
Gets on better with adults than other children			
Many fears, easily scared			
Sees tasks through to the end, good attention span			

Goodman, 1997.

Table 6.1: Mental health problems and possible interventions

Mental health problem	Intervention
Anorexia/bulimia nervosa	Family therapy, Psychotherapy, Cognitive-behaviour therapy
Anxiety	Counselling, School based group work, Behaviour therapy, Family therapy
Enuresis/encopresis	Behaviour therapy
School refusal	Behaviour therapy
Obsessional disorder	Medication, Cognitive-behaviour therapy
Reading difficulties	Psychotherapy, Counselling
Depression/grief	Psychotherapy, Counselling, Cognitive-behaviour therapy, Family therapy
Diabetes control	Psychotherapy, Counselling
Child abuse	Individual or group therapy, Parent training
Conduct disorder/aggression	Cognitive-behaviour therapy, Family therapy, Parent training, Foster care
ADHD	Social skills training, Family Therapy, Parent training, Behaviour therapy, Medication
Adjustment to divorce/separation	Counselling, Problem-solving training, Social skills training
Oppositional defiant disorder	Parent training, Behaviour therapy, Group work, Problem-solving training
Drug abuse	Family therapy, Problem solving training, Social skills training

Graham, 1996; Child Psychotherapy Trust, 1998; Carr, 2000; McNeish et al., 2002.

Table 6.2: Health of the Nation Outcome Scales (HoNOSCA)

Scale item	Section
Disruptive/aggressive behaviour	**Behaviour**
Overactivity and attentional difficulty	
Non-accidental self-injury	
Alcohol, substance/solvent misuse	
Scholastic or language skills	**Impairment**
Physical illness/disability problems	
Hallucinations and delusions	
Non-organic and somatic symptoms	
Emotional and related symptoms	
Peer relationships	**Social**
Self-care and relationships	
Family life and relationships	
Poor school attendance	
Lack of knowledge-nature of difficulties	**Information**
Lack of information-services/management	
(each scale item scored in range 0-4)	

Gowers et al., 2000.